Other Tongues

"Out of the ash
I rise with my red hair
And I eat men like air."

\-   SYLVIA PLATH, *Lazy Lazarus*

To everyone who has supported me through my battle with myself.

Parents, Friends, Strangers.

And to Tina,

For inspiring my hands with confidence to craft these pages.

Contents

The Briefest of Explanations

This is a book about the personal, internal and external experiences as a sufferer of schizoaffective disorder. Due to the formatting, which somewhat represents the mind affected by this illness, I thought it might be best to give a brief overview of the chapters and what they entail.

The Door is a sort of extended introduction that describes the contents and aims of this book more thoroughly, offering a precise insight into what the rest of the pages entail.

The Paths follows on from this, a more detailed look into what living with schizoaffective disorder is and the different routes it takes a sufferer down. The chapter includes discussions of drug abuse and sexual assault, so please be wary for triggers. As a whole it's a general overview of my life with mental illness introspectively, and how that has worsened through various decisions of my own, and others.

The Outside discusses the modern-day world and its impact on mental health; how our entire environment can be unhealthy for us and what we can do to protect ourselves from a perpetuating and incessant call of negativity from a place so vast, it could never be surprising to be a detriment to an individual's mental health.

The People, aptly named, is about the people in our lives. Those we care about and those who care for us. It's about how someone on the outside can help a sufferer of not just specifically schizoaffective disorder, but also a variety of mental health issues. It talks about how those are unwell can lift the burden on those who care for us. Perhaps most importantly, it's an acknowledgement to those who have who have suffered because of a mental health condition that was not their own, a vastly understated endeavor.

The Relapse is an acute insight to the negative effects of psychosis. It covers topics from suicide, delusion and hallucinations, so again, please be careful of triggers. This section features a lot of poetry or writings that were constructed predominantly in the midst of episodes or the experience of psychosis, offering a somewhat first-hand look at what these words actually mean. A diary, of sorts, focused on documenting the daily turmoils of this particular illness.

The Healing is the final chapter, and is centred entirely on its name. It discussed the tactics we can take forward in our journeys of recovery, methods and motivation, and sheds a little positivity after the potential bleakness of the previous chapter. It is a summation of my past year of attempted development and betterment.

So, with a few words spoken about what is to follow, the only thing to come is the following.
I hope you enjoy, or more importantly, learn.

I

<u>The Door</u>

For those I have hurt
And for those I can heal
If these words were not jumbled,
Then they would not be true,
If this seems erratic, frenzied and disorganised,
That is because it is, that is how this works
Or should I put,
Does Not.

Unqualified

Unqualified,
These presumptuous hands dictate like divinities.
A mental state that has died
Several times.
Should the mouth offer words of comfort,
When the mind feels none?
Though that mouth does still live, and does still love-
When all is said and done.
This mind may lack of expertise.
This mind may feel like reality is gone.
But in reality this mind still functions,
When all is said and done.

Metamorphoses

Definitely not an expert on psychology, or humanity, society and certainly not mental health. There is perhaps no reason for me to write this book, nor can my 'authoring' be justified as anything other than, perhaps, narcissism . I'd say if I was an expert in one thing, it would be a little flair for bad habits - and developing new, worse ones, a trait we'll discuss further over these coming pieces of dead wood. However, with the lack of expertise that I might carry, the weight of knowledge is light on these unintelligent shoulders, I can at least offer, if nothing else, introspection and insight into what the most world's most stigmatised mental health condition – what it's like to live, function and think like with this disorder.

Also, surviving.
I'd boast myself to say I've become, not an expert in, but certainly an avid pursuer of survival – my life now and this piece being testament to the above. Mental health can be the time bomb that explodes in your mind and leaves shrapnel in those around for the rest of time. Or, it can be harnessed, used, pushed into something.
Which, really, is all this is.

A Cataclysmic Concoction

To describe Schizoaffective disorder in a nutshell, it's the spicy recipe of cracking the egg of Bipolar Disorder (Depressive or Manic) into a bowl of Schizophrenia, and if you stir long enough, it can create a dangerously sour and explosive cake, that is very easily burnt. Now if that doesn't tickle your taste buds, good. The cake is horrific.

Around 3% of people hospitalised for mental health conditions in the UK suffer from Schizoaffective disorder. It's typically categorised as the combination of schizophrenia with some sort of mood disorder, which could be named negative symptoms categorised by that of the likes of depression, or symptoms more aligning with mania. So, in reality, there are these two types; depressive, or bi-polar. The latter includes an amalgamation of episodes such a hypomania, major depressive or mixed episodes, whilst the former is encapsulated by the experiences of primarily major depressive episodes. Both, of course, are categorised with the symptoms of schizophrenia.

I think the best way to explain the illness as a whole is to examine the two ingredients separately to fully grasp what's going into that nasty, nasty cake.

Symptoms that Bipolar Disorder can include (but are not limited to):

Depressive Symptoms:
- *Anxiety*
- *Long periods of a depressed state*
- *Lack of enjoyment*
- *Hopelessness*
- *Poor concentration*
- *Slow thoughts*
- *Change in appetite and weight*
- *Lack of physical energy*
- *Oversleeping/Lack of sleep*
- *Thoughts of self-harm and suicide*

Manic Symptoms:
- *Anxiety*
- *Periods of extreme energy and happiness*
- *Irritability*
- *Delusions of grandeur*
- *Impulsive decisions such as buying things, partying, promiscuous activity*
- *Lack of sleep*
- *Hearing voices*
- *Belief of having superpowers etc.*

There are differentiating variants of which Bipolar disorder into various types that a sufferer can be diagnosed with.
A Bipolar I diagnosis requires the sufferer to experience at least one full manic episode in their life, along with at least one major episode of depression in their lifetime. This is thought to affect around 1% of the population.
Bipolar II is diagnosed when a sufferer's mood swings between depressive and hypomania periods, rather than episodes of mania.
Hypomania is when a person's mood is elevated persistently over several days and can cause the person to feel confident, creative energised and productive. However, this can lead to irritability caused by other people and create disputes or conflict to erupt.
A manic episode can be brief or long periods of time (a few days up to months) that create a euphoric mood and an inflated value of self-importance, and lead to feelings of extreme grandiose. However, can also cause extreme irritability, racing thoughts and speech, lack of sleep and lack of inhibition or ability to make conducive decisions.

To give a brief of example of the difference between hypomania and a manic episode - Hypomania has made me feel great, but has also definitely made me rude to people and occasionally caused me to make self-destructive decisions, whereas Manic Episodes have made me feel fucking amazing, but completely screwed up relationships and made me think I could jump out of a 40ft building unscathed. I was far from unscathed.

Though jumping out of a window wasn't entirely mania, the event took place due to something called a Mixed State Episode, where manic and depressive symptoms appear simultaneously. I like to describe this with the funky little description of "Tired but Wired". In the window incident, I felt suicidal yet indestructible, thus leading to the idea that a 40ft fall would either hopefully kill me, or it'd be a laugh and I'd rollover and walk away with a mad adrenaline rush. No such luck. I fractured a vertebra, spent 15 days laying in a hospital bed, and then lived in a brace for 12 weeks; which really helped me nail my Robocop impersonation.

Symptoms of Schizophrenia include (but are not limited to):

- *Hallucinations (P)*
- *Delusions (P)*
- *Psychotic Experiences (P)*
- *Confused thoughts (P): Trouble keeping track of thoughts or conversations*
- *Changes in behaviour and thoughts (P): Behaving inappropriately, being unorganised or agitation*
- *Withdrawal from social situations (N)*
- *Lack of care for appearance or hygiene (N)*
- *Loss of motivation (N)*
- *Trouble concentrating (N)*
- *Decreased libido (N)*
- *Disrupted sleeping pattern (N)*

Symptoms affecting people living with Schizophrenia are typically split into two categories: positive and negative. While the title of positive symptoms might sound like a grand old time, these typically refer to a sufferer's change in thoughts or behaviors, such as experiencing auditory or visual hallucinations, or believing delusional ideas. Negative symptoms tend to impact someone in a functional or emotional context such as a withdrawal from social situations or experience "flat" emotions or apathy. In the list above, the categories are shown by "P" for positive symptoms and, you guessed it, "N" for negative.

Hallucinations can include hearing voices (most commonly), seeing nonexistent entities or smelling odors that do not exist. Auditory hallucinations can take place internally or come from outside the mind of the sufferer, can occasionally be positive although it is far more likely for these voices to be derogatory, and can comment on situations, talk about the sufferer or give commands. Most prominently for myself, the voices I experience are constant, instructing self-harm or suicide, or critiquing my weight and other aspects of appearance I am self-conscious about. Visual hallucinations might include flashes of a traumatic memory, seeing people who are not there or movement in shadows/light. Hallucinations can also affect the touch sense, such as an experience of being choked by someone when no one is there.

Delusions are beliefs held in extreme conviction even though the reality of the belief could be impossible. They can come from a feeling of paranoia, where a sufferer may believe they are being harassed or targeted by a person or group. Others can be instigated as an explanation for other symptoms. For example, I, regularly often, believe I can read people's minds due to the voices narrating what they might be thinking when I'm with someone. This can cause anxiety and links to other things that do not exist, drawing lines to dots that are on two separate pages. To use that last example, my belief is solidified by over analysing things like tone and body language in conversation, and then linked to previous unrelated experiences: "The voices say he's lying, he has his arms crossed and is looking away, and he took 3 hours to reply to my text the other night - he hates me."

Other delusions can include believing the TV is speaking directly to you, or a newspaper article was written to communicate with you alone. One specific type of delusion is referred to as the Freguli Delusion: the belief that one person is haunting the sufferer through those around them, causing extreme paranoia and distrust.

An acute psychotic experience, or episode, is not fun for anyone. They can cause excruciatingly drastic changes in behaviour and thoughts, creating anxiety, distrust, anger and distress for those experiencing it. During the episode the sufferer can go through emotional turmoil, experience extreme perceptual disturbances from hallucinations, and go through delusions that may cause them to reject help. This can be incredibly difficult to cope with for those around and those close to them. As an example, one of my recent major psychotic episodes started over an hour period after a lovely day, and the next thing I knew I was sitting on the side of a road, voices manifesting inside me and crying prejudice and hate, thinking somebody was trying to kill me, and I should kill myself so they couldn't do it, while a friend tried to talk me out and (eventually successfully) took me to hospital.

There is an estimate that around 0.3% of the population experience schizoaffective symptoms during their lives, and that a third of schizophrenia diagnoses are classified as the aforementioned illness. Due to its nature of having many overlapping symptoms with other illnesses, it can prove to be very difficult to diagnose, particularly as it has a tendency of impacting different people in various ways. Some believe that the disorder, as a whole, is more common in women but men are more likely to develop it earlier in life. The actual causes are relatively unknown, but there are possible routes such as genetics, environmental development and trauma that could spark traits of psychosis. However, that isn't what this is about.

Ultimately, I am not going to give you hours of research and objective facts. This is merely how this mind works. Or doesn't, to be precise. Overactive in all of the ineffective areas that could be conducive to a healthy life.

Genetics

Blood in the roots,
Makes the tree grow sick
But this is not your fault,
No one can be expected to hold blame.
Illness does not travel in a second name,
It is individual. It is developed with life,
Through all of its mediocrity, turmoil's and it's strife.
So, hold no guilt for this head that I hold,
And I will bear no shame when I am old.
Even if every silver lining contains a cloud,
It does not mean I cannot touch life's medals that shine gold.

The Set Up

Today a decision was made, amongst the shouting and retching of voices, the soaring and plummeting of mood swings and the stillness and shaking of anxiety, to create. To create a routine of creation. To create a routine, in which the purpose is creativity, to create a creation of creative proportions.

The idea catalysed itself last night, at a friend's, as I smoked out of her window while she worked, fairy lights and a lamp dimly lighting a room containing a plethora of art and inspiration, I thought about the interview we had done earlier. The interview is to provide relevant (and irrelevant) muses for a song I am to write with my band, about what it means to care for someone with mental sickness. This friend has supported me through some of my worst times, and has witnessed my worst moments, from volcanic levels of mania seeping out of my skin, to the most paralysing psychotic episodes of my life. I knew I had to write about this person.

So, two hours later, I'm still thinking about one of her answers. A question of how to make it easier for yourself when caring, and advice to a carer.

"I take time to myself" - or something along those lines, I am horrific for misquoting.

Nevertheless, it was an excruciatingly simple statement that stuck with me.

Something I had never really considered before, as I pressed her for details, was to do something even if it meant doing nothing, for myself.

Which is where I find myself now.

Now obviously, I mean that much less melodramatic than it sounds, but here we are now.

Phone off, a new "no distractions" writing app downloaded, a cup of chamomile and yoga soundscapes playing softly (though just loud enough to overdub my flat mates singing from down the hall).

I intent to write every day until completion, whatever my mental state, as I refuse to give the false impression that I have recovered from the breaking in my mind - this will be an honest insight.
In hope, this will be a new chapter.
A glimpse into the reality of Schizoaffective Disorder.
This is an offering of information and experience.
A handshake.
In reality, well, we'll see if anything comes to fruition.

II

The Paths

To the Thieves of Sound,
To the devils that forced my mouth shut, but could never contain
my words.

Rebirth

I hate phrases
Such as A New Chapter,
Or Turning the Page
As if it is so simple
And the events of the Book so far,
Have been unimportant, until now.
However,
With that said
I am beginning the first chapter
Of my second book
In the saga that is life
Relive.
Relapse.
Redo.
Release.
Rebirth.

Instigation

As far as I can remember, my first experience of psychotic symptoms began at around the age of twelve. I remember over the course of several weeks, the volume and intensity of hearing voices in my head increased - a jarring experience. For some time, I assumed it was a perfectly normal part of life, maybe even a part of the dreaded puberty phase. I would see lights that rippled across walls and seemed to want to direct me places, to guide me to some unknown destination. By the age of fourteen, the voices I could hear were very near to constant, and entirely derogatory. My life at school was never horrific, of course I had problems like any other teenager, but I did relatively well in most classes and had a reasonable group of friends - alongside a group of definitely-not-friends. However, as whispers in my skull began to overtake my thoughts it became much more difficult to concentrate in class, to get up in the morning, or to even have conversations with those I enjoyed being around. I was part of a youth theatre at the time that was of great help in allowing me to express myself and have a creative outlet, but still I didn't feel anyone understood me, nor could I be totally open about the issues I was having - largely due to the fact I did not understand them myself. I, at some point during this time, began self-harming in an attempt for some sort of release from the mental pain - as sadly, many others in my generation have done, including a fair few of my peers at the time. I was referred, I think by a teacher at school, to a GP where I was then referred to a teenage psychiatric ward in Dundee. This involved an eight-month waiting list, followed by 6 weeks (my choice) of talking therapy. After two weeks, I had decided I no longer wanted to take part in these conversations - I had no trust in the doctor I saw, and I think I expected more immediate results in healing.

Thus, over the following 4 weeks I displayed signs of immaculate recovery, feigning my progress and deceiving those aiding me in order to be left alone - which worked well. I was discharged, and I realised my capacity for lying. Something which would become a huge detriment to my future relationships - and a common trait among people diagnosed with schizoaffective disorder. I didn't realise that was a problem for around 6 years post.

I had never really noticed the isolation of mental illness until this point. Maybe there was a subconscious comfort in thinking everybody around me felt the same. You only notice your differences when they are pointed out. Shame ensued, as did distrust. I'd even argue it catalysed other symptoms.

Unthought Problems

Living with Schizoaffective Disorder has its problems. Some
obvious, some not. Hollywood has tarted up the illness to form a
gang of psychopathic murderers who want to kill their parents
and then themselves. To name names, films such as Split and
Shutter Island have both pointed the big blame finger towards
psychosis and dissociative disorders, and this history of
stigmatisation in the film industry can be seen as far back as
Hitchcock's 'Psycho', where the horror flicks antagonist is
explained with stereotyped diagnosis and an outdated Oedipus
complex.

 People living with these disorders are still human. We can still
function, to varying degrees. I'd like to take a moment to
address any screenwriter who might have used the phrase
'Paranoid Schizophrenic' as a way to explain the actions of any
cruel, sadistic or inhumane characters in their work. With all
due respect - you are a shameless, lazy writer. This antagonises
a vast group of individuals in the name of a quick profit.
Of course, many symptoms can be as horrific in real life as they
are portrayed in films - usually more so. Filmed media's will
sadly never have the capability to give an accurate experience of
a psychotic episode. Not even modern-day virtual reality
technology can ever achieve this - it fails on two conditions.
1) A VR set is used voluntarily.
2) It can be switched off when desired.

This sadly has led us to the belief where we must rely on the way mental illness is portrayed through the mediums, we have access to, with limited results. Albeit, research and empathy can help imagine the experiences of hearing voices and hallucinating visual - but no individual soul, bar those that have been cursed, can ever witness or gain the knowledge of what these weighted terms are defined by. We can all imagine what some hallucinations might feel like. You may have tried psychedelics. You may recall the feeling of hearing someone whisper your name when no one did, or your phone buzzing in your pocket but alas, no one has text (This is a sign of mobile addiction and if you experience this you should probably cut down on social media), and sympathy may give some insight to the more obvious symptoms. However, some problems might not be as obvious as others, so here's a list of problems that people might not realise.

"You don't seem schizophrenic" - No one does.

Antipsychotics: What an atrocious name for a medication. Of course, the name is what it does on the tin, but the stigma of a name such as this is severely stigmatised that people can have judgmental reactions to. The word psychotic has connotations that are ill portrayed in the media. Psychosis is not what you see in films. It is not portrayed accurately in media. It is definitely more common in the world than most realise, and definitely more common than most want to realise.

High Functionality: I have good days, not every day starts with waging war with the duvet to get out of bed. It is naive to think people with mental illness are unable to function. Often, they can, and often they can't. Every diagnosis is a differentiating spectrum. There is no one Anxiety, just like there is no one way to break your leg. Of course, every 24 hours that pass bring its own spectrum. One hour may be spent in delusion, 20 minutes in extreme mania, and then 3 hours of working or relaxing like anyone else. There are no confinements, nor restrictions, on the amount of time a disorder can impact someone daily. Nor is there limitation on how destructive, or conducive, that period may be. One hour. One month. Three Minutes. Thirteen weeks. There are both short term, long term, and everlasting symptoms that spring throughout the illnesses career.

Attention from Professionals: It is difficult to get doctors to listen. Or to even get help in the first place. I made an attempt at my life before I was seen by anyone professionally, but they didn't hear me when I said I couldn't make it through the length of a waiting list. It's hard to get help until the last second, which is sadly the state of the NHS and funding. However, then many doctors will put words in your mouth or will be unable to help unless certain words or answers come up, such as "I am suicidal". People need help before then.

Reactions: Episodes, of any variety, can be abnormal to most people. But they are normal for many of us. Please don't treat someone having a panic attack like a zoo animal, and please don't let the flat mate screaming at the imaginary man suffer alone. It can be hard and awkward to offer help, but acts of kindness are needed. Sometimes episodes are not even required to deter the eyes of people. Simply acting 'off' or 'being different' can be enough to upset someone's gaze and evoke the word 'freak' to protrude from their tongue. Judgements are noticed and they amplify internal struggles. A smile might bring some calm to a relentless void. Judge less, process more, forgive more.

Media Consumption: It's not new for people to be stressed by modern life, especially with how it is portrayed in the media. Everyone is scared of turning on the news or comparing themselves to Instagram models. Monsters lurk behind every screen - from fake beauty designed to degrade and shame us or fear of our dying planet/society/fucking everything in the world right now. But other mediums can be hard. When I listen to a podcast, sometimes I can get confused as to where the people are hiding, or I can begin to believe that it is I, who have been sent to save Private Ryan. Some nights I tear my room apart searching for the radio the government placed in the wall, others I believe a singer's lyrics about me - the fear is near constant. Does the author know about my childhood?

Guilt: I am aware I can be difficult. Depressive episodes can be isolating in company, even when aware of the effect you're having on a group. You can be boring, lazy. let people down or just not good company. Mania can be the opposite, too loud, talking over people, inability to listen coherently, talking in tangents, being blunt about personal trauma in a humorous way. Then after a while, a drip into depression can happen. Psychosis can be upsetting and confusing for a witness, and can be demanding on their mental strength. Psychosis can take away awareness, create irritability and lack of judgement, paranoia. It impacts those around. Episodes are like time-bombs that explode in your mind, and leave shrapnel in those who care. Existence can feel like an everlasting erosion to the hearts of those around - it aches my soul too. I am trying. I am trying. I am trying. I am.

Everyday bring its own new struggles with psychosis. From relatively small issues such as a roller-coasting libido or sporadic diet, to fugue states of waking in places you didn't fall asleep, with voices reminiscent of hell screaming for your absence. Confusion is perhaps the biggest player in the chess game of relations. There have been often occasions of miss-remembrance or forgetfulness that have strung throughout friendships - or even more damaging then this, hallucinatory concoctions of events that never happened, but with every moment and emotion recalled as if every second had been real. These moments of fabrication can range from tiny insignificant times, or cataclysmic events that could change life forever. There are rarely grey areas with this disorder. Life is often just monochromatic. Differentiation is difficult.

Benjamin

Who are you?
Where did you come from?
How did those chains come to be?
Placed around your wrists, for only me to see?
Have you ever washed your hair?
Have those endless, black vipers ever been cut?
Or have they continued to grow, relentlessly,
Ever since you ran out of luck?
Did you pick me?
Or were you forced?
Did they send you?
Or were you coerced
With money, or drugs,
Or was it plain sadism?
Oh, Wraith dressed in satin,
Why did you come to me?

I feel you watch me at night,
Your glare frozen and heavy.
I steal glances of your silhouette
Your pose always poised, and ready.
I could never hurt you,
For I know you are a ghost.
But until you reveal your face to me,
I'll never know who haunts me most.

Why the fuck did you come for me?
I guess you'll never tell.
Was it even me that named you?
Or was it those black angels who birthed you, in the lowest
parts of hell?
Oh angel, I still see you
And I can smell you in my dreams
I hear you breathe, so spitefully
That I am fearful of your schemes
Oh Benjamin, Oh Benjamin

I pray, explain your origin
For you make me fear that in my own head,
I am an unwelcome foreigner.
That you should be me,
I should be you,
And I can sense how much you hate me,
Tell me, please.
What, in your honor, am I to do?

A List of Things That Make Me Cry (That Probably Shouldn't)

Having to choose clothes in the morning.
Speaking in front of groups of people.
Writing about certain things. Ranging from trauma to Birthday
Cards.
Winnie the Pooh. Consistently.
Upsetting others.
Being in busy elevators.
Plans getting cancelled.
Not having a rough time schedule for the day.
Cooking disappointing food.
Running out of coffee.
The fact that Yorkshire Puddings have eggs in them.
Losing my water bottle. Or other objects that shouldn't be
sentimental.
Great concept albums.
Out of the blue texts from friends.
Breaking a routine.
Rude bouncers.
Seeing my cats on FaceTime.
Reading/watching the News.
A nice hug.
Something inconvenient happening between 17:00 and 20:00.
Getting a significant tattoo.
People's tone of voice and body language.
Not being able to wash.
Loud pubs.
Dead artists.
Angry men.
Feeling out of control of my own life.
People being nice.
Thoughtful Presents.
Foxes.
Successful opportunities.
Any sort of praise.
Assessments.
Endings.

A Masterclass in Mind Reading

Since the age of 12 I have been hearing voices in my head, all people I know in real life speaking to me inside my mind. Whether the individual has had a positive or negative impact on my life, they reside in the corners of my mind, rent free, offering truth.

When I say offering truth, I mean people cannot bullshit me. When I was 14, I started getting really interested in aspects of psychology which has further developed over the years, but at that time I became fascinated by non-verbal communication and how vocal quality and word choices conveys what we think, even if it is unintentional. As an insecure teenager I read several books, watched documentaries and read research into studies that showed results on how we communicate with tools out-with our usual vocabulary - to my detriment. At the time I took every word I processed in my research as a set of infallible laws that every human being adhered to in conversation, leading to my belief that I could tell people word choice was not working alongside their thought process. Combined with the voice of present company's voice in my head, I suddenly felt I had the ability to read minds: I read the tell-tale signs, and the voices confirmed my suspicions.

Fast forward six years and this is the same, albeit to a (thankfully) lesser extent. Rules in tone and non-verbal communication are not gold dust, which I have found relatively easy to distinguish when comparing a conversation with my own paranoia. However, when you walk through a shop and hear every customer's opinion of you, when you make your purchase and can hear the cashier judging you for buying full fat hummus instead of low, the problem persists.

While I have been able to reduce this delusion down to an idea, the idea still proceeds. I regularly find myself mistrusting the words of others, trusting my own instinct (or the instinct of a mental illness) over what is more likely truth. I have strategies to help me process what might be fact from my fantasy. If I hear a voice and the associated owner is not looking at me, it is my paranoia. If someone's actions go against the intentions I hear, it is my paranoia.

Sadly, however, I to do this day cannot trust compliments. A combination of my own self-esteem, illness and the intensity of the "thought hearing" in these scenario's creates unease, discomfort and disbelief. Words hold a great deal of weight, and I am not of the belief that I deserve, or others can believe, thoughts about myself that contradict my own.

While now I know (most of the time) I am not a mind reader, I cannot trust words. Words are used for deception. Actions are honest. If you want to earn trust, you have to show it, not tell it.

Gifted

Doctors proclaim a symptom
But I proclaim Gifted,
The voices in my head or not solely in my mind.
But they are in your brain too, acting as my spies
You hear not their whispers, but they hear all of yours
And report them back to me
So, I can know for certain, when your lips tell lies,
Your internal reactions,
I feel them too
And when your smile is fake
I can see through
I know what you think
And I know what you feel
You cannot dissuade me
For I know what is real,

Doctors say medicate
I say A Higher Mental State,
Aware of toxicity and false claims
A double-edged sword which can cause distress,
But also, liberty
From the snakes and the vultures, I am free
From words of poison and two-faced spite
I will not let them associate with me,

Doctors suggest paranoia,
But I suggest Jealousy.
That they cannot read me as easily,
As I to them
And while they know not my words instigators,
I know from where their thoughts stem,

Doctors diagnose 'delusional',
But I diagnose 'Gifted'.

Working on It

I used to believe I had to destroy myself to entice other people
Now I destroy myself to entice some self-erotic egotism.
Self-destruction is addictive for the rush of survival,
The ability to hide, it is a pestilence of pleasant thriving.
It's 3 steps backwards, but each step forward feels beautifully
gratifying.
And thus, I keep stepping back.

No longer. I step one pace. I follow with the other foot. I stand
tall.
Only one pace. But one pace nonetheless.

<u>Catalysts</u>

A list of things that cause mood swings:

- Anything
- Nothing

Compulsive Thinking

It doesn't leap to falsify radical conclusions - it's an ever-evolving and logical step-by-step process in which the menial becomes cataclysmal. The feather turns to the brick in a perfectly fashioned process, every detail of the progression makes absolute sense - even if the overall picture may seem skewed. The adaptation of thoughts from harmony to disjunction takes mere moments. In some ways, anxiety may make the greatest detective known to the world, if only those races of thought led to accurate conclusions.

This is the problem with overthinking - the conclusion may seem ludicrous and laughable, but the journey of ideas from which the conclusion was conceived rarely seems anything but infallible. The brain seems to make 40 split second decisions in the time of a blink - faster when under pressure, with the distances of each leap varying considerably and their plot line twisting and turning based on fear. Compulsive overthinking stems from fear then, surely? It is the idea and paranoia of a thousand "what ifs" in a singular, rapidly shifting stream of consciousness that avoids any sense of conscientious rationality. The pathway of anxiety is that of a long, looming corridor with walls that stretch beyond sight, scraping more than just the sky or the clouds, but the very fabrics of space. They loom, intimidatingly over our small and nervous skeletons as we are forced to believe the only explanation is to sprint down this corridor of melancholia, with heart pounding and sweat soaking our very souls as we run, and run, and run. Vicious walls decorated with our memories and trauma's race us on either side, closing in, and it is impossible not to notice the pictures that most appeal to our fear induced fantasies - the images that flash in duality with what our minds are already scared of. The corridor ends, eventually, leaving us with new explanations that we picked up in our panic, from those most vivid portraits of terror that haunted our running track.

What we failed to realise before sprinting down those overfilled halls, was our perspective. In front lies fear and lack of focus. And in that fear, when it beckoned, we ran towards it, our mind racing faster than our bodies, finding conclusion and evidence in its adrenaline infused search for space. We never thought to turn around. Maybe behind, mere steps away, the walls and walkway are shorter, the decorations barren and unobtrusive. A shorter, calmer stroll. A viewpoint to assess and review accurately.

It is exceedingly difficult to never jump to conclusions, overthink or put oneself into a panic - maybe our brains or bodies enjoy the rush. However, it is imperative to living a slightly-less-troubled life that we learn how to reframe our anxieties, to take a step back and focus with realism rather than let our imaginations take the reins of our hearts, leading us to chaos. Step back and analyse. Step forward with a plan.

Airwaves

I spoke with aliens yesterday. Well, received contact from. As I sat in the garden with cigarettes and Plato for company, I heard them. In my left ear, a definitive trebly sound - almost like some sort of wobbling synthesizer playing for me. When I turned my head, it disappeared. A natural sound would have followed my sense, surely.
It lasted only a minute and I had to keep my head statue-like. I could feel it as some sort of transmission meant for me, one I have thus far been unable to decipher. A code, a language, a call. I don't know. Perhaps some sort of invitation that only the future can define. I will keep my eyes, ears and mind open, ready for the next signal. I have no doubt they will be back. I cannot afford to make any mistakes over the coming weeks, in case they are watching. I hope writing this is not heresy to them. Call again soon, please.
Give me more.

Sleep

How people sleep in a healthy routine consistently will always remain to be an unsolved mystery to me. Why aren't they worrying? Aren't you thinking of what you should be doing while you're in bed? How does your body allow more than 4 hours rest?

Lack of sleep will decline your mental health. Your mental health may decrease your ability to sleep. What a vicious little circular dickhead. Oversleeping might become a thing, the inability to leave bed or even wake up.
Either or, you're tired. It's shit. You're in pain because you need to rest so badly.

This little routine helped me for a while. Try this for the next 3 days. Maybe you'll benefit a little.

Set an alarm early morning. Let's say 8am. If you're awake at 5am, you still need to get up at 8am. It doesn't matter if it's your day off. Put your alarm on the other side of the room, with a glass of water next to it. When it goes off, do not turn off the alarm until you have finished the whole glass. Now do a big stretch, and leave the room for at least 15 minutes. Maybe shower, maybe exercise, maybe write, maybe just go for a smoke, just get away from the bedroom.
When you feel a little more awake, you can go back in. Not until then.
Do this for a few days. It doesn't matter if you're still not nodding off until the morning, eventually your body will realise it cannot sustain itself on that little amount of sleep. You should start to get tired earlier and hopefully sleep for longer. It can even feel good to be up early and get on with the day, however painfully those first 30 seconds (2 hours) are.

If you're lying in bed for ages, stop it. Get out and do something else. The act of consciously trying to sleep will most likely wake you up more than most activities.

Try and stay away from screens before bed. If you can't, making get some amber tinted UV glasses.

Focus on your breathing, if you can't concentrate and have a budget, try a Dodow (a sleep metronome designed by insomniacs) to prompt you into a relaxing rhythm of breath.

Exercise earlier in the day.

Don't go to bed hungry.

Try a couple of days without caffeine.

Do not nap. If you're tired during the day, have a glass of water and some chewing gum. Don't lie down.

Seek professional help. Look into CBT for Insomnia/Sleep Disturbance.

If you're body isn't sleeping, it may not feel the need to yet. Spend time on something not strenuous that won't grab your attention too fixedly. Occupy your mind on something until it starts to feign, you cannot force the opportunity to sleep, as much as we all want to.

Don't punish yourself for not sleeping, if it was your choice, you would. Your body just might not be ready for that yet, as much as you want it to be. It's a waiting game. A painful, tedious and aggravating waiting game, but one you can eventually conquer.

Nightmares

The duvet sometimes, often, speaks
It whispers in the cold, in the harsh quiet:
"Let me comfort you",
And when I am wrapped in its radiating cloth,
Safety becomes an option.
Warmth becomes true and ice melts away,
For short respite.
But soon after it tangles knots around limbs
Muscles are nothing against these waves
That twist and toil and never relinquish,
In the name of comfort.
I can no longer sleep.
If I sleep, I fear
My bed will be the death of me.

Prodigal Father

Today a hero of mine passed through this life via his own hand. The sensation of numbness that overcame me following the news was overbearing. He was a musician of poise and intent, an inspiration to the way my own hand pens it's lyrical phrases. When I first began writing poetry, I would write for his band's instrumentation, my delivery motivated by his passion, my content and rage the child of his.

Maybe we are so far inclined to our heroes because we believe the masks that are worn in the media - what newspaper or magazine ever asks an interviewee if they are stable, if they are happy, if they are comfortable? Perhaps our system of journalism needs to feature the person, not the highlights. We are drawn by stories, not mentality - are we satisfied by this? Media can support artists without being intrusive, perhaps through more privacy, or through genuine concern. But what industry contains any authentic concern for its workers anymore?

Creative expression is no guarantee of mental cleansing. The mouths exhalation of the vocabulary is not equal to the mind's purification. 'Getting things off of one's chest' is not always relief, it is sometimes merely an admittance of virus.
Words can dilute but not cure. An appeal: if you are the consumer of anyone's expression, listen to what they express. There are under laying cries for help all over that go unrecognized and unhealed. Countless minds are lost every day all over, and while facts are produced of this, they are not noted by most. Anyone means ANY person. Be gentle, be kind, be open.

Breathe.

Loss will forever be a part of life. Death is the necessity for new life. It brings pain, grief, aggravation, dark temptation and loss of sensation. It also brings knowledge, growth, clarity. When you inevitably lose someone in life remembrance will guide your way. Look for facts in confusion, contentment in disgust, seconds of light in days of black.

Liar, Liar

Power of this tongue,
Snake of teetering love and endless toils,
The blood on my hands, the hearts I hath spoiled,
Through lust of my lips and the souls I have ripped
With syllables uttered with no thought,
I never even admitted the tales you never bought.
My vocal cords spit cancer,
On the highest heresies I appear as a dancer,
Wide limbs and static explosions,
With my teeth, to our faith I wrought erosion.

Honest Living

The vitality of honesty cannot be stressed enough in the discussion of mental health; honesty with loved ones, friends, doctors, and even yourself, is absolutely crucial in order to engage in the process of recovery, or coping, with any sort of turmoil in life. Admission is everything in the beginning - no problem cannot be fought without some grounds of acknowledgment, but it must be kept up to ensure the persistence of healthy change.

To begin, it is unfair to those around us, especially to those we love or who love us, to not be honest with the places we are in. Facades of who we are can never be kept up if they are untrue, and will always break eventually. This eventual reluctance of the truth can harm and betray those we hold in mutual trust - this, I have learned through experience. We must be open and frank, as hard as it may be, to those who seek to help us, or who may even just be affected by our states. It is always better to be honest and offer preparation for the worst times, than for those around us to find out through some worse and more painful channel.

Sometimes honesty has the appearance of being un-charming, and trivial. Not that it is difficult to be honest (though of course, with many things it is), but more in that there is no appeal to it, it seems to hold a pointlessness to it. This has been a common thought when I am most unwell. I strive for it to not be so. I think I am succeeding. But maybe I'm just not being honest with myself.

Compulsion

As previously mentioned, compulsive lying is a frequent trait among those diagnosed with schizoaffective disorder. Lying is not as simple in these scenario's however - falsities can easily be confused with delusion. Moments of intent and lack of clarity are easily muddled with each other. This easily leads to a 'boy who cried wolf' situation.

I find it difficult to talk about the lies I have told - due to the disgust I now hold for myself. I know for myself, in certain scenario's that I had no idea I was lying, but in other's I am fully aware that I had intent to attempt to direct, manipulate for misuse words for my own gain. To those I have told mis-truths to, I am so deeply sorry.

I like to think it is a bad habit I have now conquered, and I now process, think and deliver every sentence with far more intent and honesty than ever before. But I will never be able to undo the strings I dealt in the past. I am sorry for the relationships I ruined, for the friends I hurt, and for the trusts I broke.

I am trying.

I am aware now.

Lying builds like any other habits. It offers power and smugness for a short while - always followed by guilt, regret and self-loathing. False words are never worth their consequences. Syllables are precious, the weight of words can never be stressed enough. Never let your tongue be tempted from truth - it will only bring misery, for all.

Tuesdays

I can't sleep. There's something about this 24-hour period that fuels me with rage. From the stroke of 11:59 Monday evening my skin starts to crawl, my mind racing to some destination I can never place. I am unsure of where I when this started. It's as if my brain turns into a spider, with each leg sprinting in a different direction, all at different paces and all in varying durations of rapidity. I squeeze my eyes and attempt to seize control of my breath, bring myself into the meditative state I have grown so comfortable in - but I can never locate that safe space. I am dragged through wakening nightmares and anguish, every thought birthed from some forgotten paranoia. If I am able to feign some sort of rest it is tormented with visions of perplexity and instigations - I am repeatedly the villain in some mystifying plot.

Awakened, things are no different. Anxiety and rage coarse my blood like a starving dog that has been offered its first meal in weeks, but tortures itself in attempt to pick its poison. I pace and writhe around my room, searching for respite, unable to place my mind, or body, upon any sort of settlement. I focus all desires into a task for 15 minutes a piece. A hugely engorged quarter of an hour - something that feels productive, motivated. And then the time ends, the frustration ensues and the time is realised to be wasted, tormenting me thus even further. The crevices of my skull scream. I can feel shouting behind my eyes, and my ears feel plugged, my mouth stitched. How did it come to this? What is it about this day that brings anguish without fail? Anguish and misery, made in psychosis' secrecy. The other's in the head are keeping something from me. Antagonising me. I can feel it, even if I cannot see. I wish I could reap their codes and crack their enigma, yet the more I push the more my hair is torn out by my own hands. It's hard to control a self-made prophecy of planning and schedules when others connive and scheme against you.

Every week, without fail. I lose a piece. A part of control on myself. It is wearing me down. I struggle to bare this any further. Next Tuesday is only 6 days away, again.

Scarring

Please be warned, this section delves into discussion about sexual assault and abuse.

Notes on Trauma

No one in this world has lived without some kind of trauma occurring in their life. That is the tragic state of our world, but more tragically is that most of us forget that. Or more directly, most of us forget we can be traumatised. We live in a world where Political Correctness has never been more spoken of, but juxtaposed with extreme opposition to this. For every feminist there are ten anti-feminists trolling through twitter. For every mental health advocate, there are 30 people still referring to the 'loony bin'. Words burn.
For every comedian that can make us laugh without verbally abusing anyone, there are a hundred that resort to jokes of racism and rape. If you can't make jokes without aiming at someone, you're not funny.

I digress into this as I think as a society, we need to be far more vigilant in our efforts to be aware. We need to label more clearly things that could seriously distress a person going through a battle with trauma and recovery. A person recovering from anorexia might be triggered by a TV show that uses fat jokes as it's reoccurring punchline or the exposure we have to Photoshopped model's bodies - expectations that no one can achieve, hence the Photoshop. I don't want to see Brad on twitter talking about how 'schiz' his ex was for shouting at him (when he cheated on her) and I don't enjoy almost every movie villain being referred to in some sort of way as mentally ill. There is a notion that being hurt by something makes you a 'delicate snowflake'. That if you're offended by something your opinion is tainted and invalid. We need to become the delicate blizzard. Instead of people negating their feelings in a world of repression and toxic masculinity we need to express them, express that being hurt comes from somewhere. If your words have hurt someone, you are the problem, not the person who has been hurt. That's just a class A example of victim blaming. The world as a whole must improve, we have more information and research on mental health and social injustice than ever before so people need to read that information. We need to care about our fellow humans, and not ridiculed them for being justifiably upset. It wouldn't be censoring if it was just a show of empathy. We need to be more aware. Sadly however, awareness doesn't sell.

Now I've finished my social political rant (although I can promise more later), it's time to discuss trauma.

.

At the age of 18 I was raped by a man more than double my age. He was a friend.

Was.

Now, was.

It was the single most destructive moment of my life. It tore my brain in two. I have never felt so helpless, or weak, or puny, or small, or disgusting, or dirty as that night. There's nothing more degrading and nothing more painful. That night I did not sleep, I did not speak, I did not move. I just sat by the toilet, the occasional tear falling down my cheek, and throwing up every time I was able to. His words had multiplied his actions. The insults he spat on me.
I bought into every single one of them.

For a while afterwards, he continued to message me as if nothing had happened.
'It was a drunk thing'.
I was drunk as well; I didn't feel the need to abuse him. I stayed in touch with him because I wanted to believe he wasn't a monster. But he was. It took me around 18 months to finally ensure he could no longer contact me. I don't know why, maybe I was romanticising him, maybe I was waiting for him to say something that erase it all. Of course, nothing ever could.

For the first couple of weeks my life continued as normal. I went to college as normal the next day. I made a joke of it, that a 43-year-old man had tried to come on to me. It was a funny lie, it made light of it for me while being able to half express an element of what had happened.
Six months later I had my first breakdown and told someone. Around twelve months later I was still having breakdowns, but had my first one at work. I worked for my parents, and had to vaguely explain, through tears and terror.
It was strange, being so fine and then suddenly not. I guess that's what repression does, viciously.

Youth

As I write through turmoil and tears
I am reminded of your grin
The thick accent that directed
Your requests
Your instructions
Your demands
You had your way
You took trust away
But not from Us
You took My trust
My faith
The final straw
In the wary structure of those I had hope in.

As your hand closed like a Venus fly trap
You devoured your prey
When I was in joy
And joy has never turned to such paralysis
And now I fear joy
Just as I fear love
As I thought, for a while
That's what you were showing me

It was a body you craved
It was a mind you fucked
For the rest of its patchwork life.

Relationships & Sex

Breathe.
Be open early.
Identify red areas.
Do not cross boundaries.
Never accept anything less than comfort.
Believe and trust your partner.
Let them teach you love.
Learn and release.
Practice, slowly.
Make sure you are entirely in control, until you are comfortable enough to relinquish that.
Wait.
Breathe.
Admire the purity of their body. Adore the purity of their mind.
Remember the purity of your body. Remember the purity of your mind.
Don't focus on mistakes, adapt and progress.
Breathe.
You probably won't get it right first time. That's okay.

Remember you never have to.

Giving & Receiving

Always give the out the love you want to feel, focus on the other person entirely. Do not dwell on dreams of the future or your idea of what the relationship with them could be. Focus on them in the present, be with them, react and hear them. Do not value your needs over theirs. It's okay to make sacrifices for each other or involving each other. Your lives are not intertwined, merely close by. Do not allow a relationship to be an excuse to neglect yourself. Do not allow yourself to neglect a relationship. Love bravely. Be ready to fight for it. Try and fix problems. Listen and adapt. Speak your mind and hear theirs. Love unconditionally. Allow yourself to feel that love. Accept the others feelings, for the good and the bad - do not try and change them. Respect every decision. Help each-other when possible, but do not place sole dependence on the other. I have learned these too late from my own mistakes.
Everyone makes mistakes.
Accept.
Develop,
Grow.

Different Lips

Her wholeness
In the hole you left
Filling a void
And a feeling of dread
The sweetness and smell of her hair
Took away the blood and stench of your sweat
Her healing light
On the bruises you left in darkness
Her care
On the body you so gently ravaged
Her delicacy
Your brutality
Her whisper
Your shout
Her calm
Your rage
Her whisper
You lose
You lost
You will not win me again
I learned love's true definition,
When she could have made my body hers
But instead made it my own

Letting It Scar

Do not repress. Feel. Witnessing your own paid and letting it
flow through you is the only way to process what has happened
to you. When you are cut you must bleed before you can scar.
The scar may never fade, but it may only be a mark on the
surface. Perhaps even unnoticeable. But seek help to feel.

After my succession of breakdowns post-trauma, I undertook
EMDR therapy via a private psychotherapist. For the first time
therapy, or a doctor, helped me. EMDR works (in a far more
sophisticated way than I can explain) by breaking down patterns
in your brain such as things that might connect trauma. For
instance, I couldn't allow anyone to touch my neck, the slightest
pressure (from a finger to having a top button done up) caused a
panic attack and all too vivid memories of being choked. The
therapy was difficult. It was emotional and took me back. But I
moved through it, the chemical reactions were broken and now I
can feel pressure all over the area - within reason. Nightmares
slowly started to fade and the paranoia that He was following
me wherever I went finally crept away.

Not always, of course. I still have fear and I still have panic
attacks, he still creeps up in psychosis and thinking of him
always brings on a mood swing. But I think about him less. He
intrudes less. I am aware more. I can control myself more. And I
laugh more.

You need to let yourself bleed, without bleeding out. You need to let the bleeding be external, no one can help if they cannot see the wound. Drink water after panic attacks. Set boundaries when you are talking, make sure you guide the conversation and don't feel the need to answer questions - only say what you want to and are comfortable with. Breathe. If you don't trust someone, don't, but tell. I couldn't open up to a doctor for a long time as he fit the profile of the man who harmed me. If I had told someone that something new could have been arranged easily, rather than the excruciating 20 minutes of panic and silence I had whenever I met him. Try yoga, or meditation. If you're thinking about the event, generalise it. Do not torture yourself on details. Some details will stick out more, demand attention like history demands respect - make them apart of the haze to forget. It's easier to desensitise a general event than it is one action, so when you do think only of the synopsis of what happened to you, don't analyse it frame by frame. Cook for yourself and a loved one, and believe it when they admire it. Be kind to yourself. No one deserves trauma. And those who do suffer it need more support from themselves than any amount another can give. Only you can claim back your freedom.

If nobody knows, tell one person. It will be difficult, but it's a start that will snowball. Even if you don't feel better and don't tell anyone else, you will be more comfortable knowing someone see's you through a better lens than anyone else.

Do not apologise for what happened to you.
Do not apologise for how it has made you feel.

Fight it. If not for love of yourself, for the spite of those who hurt you.
Spite the red in hope of the light.

Adrenaline

Did you mean to engrave yourself on me?
Did you think it would be a one-off occurrence?
That I'd feel only pain in the present moment,
And never recall the tearing and crashing,
The crying and the thrashing,
The tears and the grins,
Did you think I could relinquish those moments?
They grip tighter than a noose,
Handcuffs from which I will never break loose.
Did you expect a different circumstance?
Where I could stand comfortably and watch you dance?
Do you remember,
Do you?
Do you miss it?
I'll not lie I've not felt the same rush,
As when you're claws tore limbs from my hair
Of when I could tell the intent of your glare,
The pain. The lust.
You fucker.
I've never felt such a rush.

The 'One More' Mind Set

Here we are.
A brown belt.
A tablespoon filled with tar.
I've let go and it never so good.
A new perspective.
Die. Let live.
I found perspective on the ground.
Laying down, lost in psychedelic sounds.
We dance.
I ask,
"Do cigarettes and ketamine give you substance?"
I fall.
You answer something remorse with profound unintelligibility.
The ground is cold, my blood warm
The sun fills my body as I am torn
Between the idea of moving and the thought of comfort.
That's the thing about a habit:
The comfort.
The serenity.
The intensity.
Take the hit, feel less shit and leave the pit of
Doubt and Shame
Forget
You are the only one to blame
For this mess
People that care - they stress
They have no fucking idea where you are.
Your arm starts to scar and peel
And in withdrawal you wish you could never feel again.
But there's one thing you want to feel.
Take another hit
Watch Dragon's Den, off your face.
Put Theo Paphitis into place.
A friend calls. Ignore.
A doctor calls. Ignore.

Who needs help,
When you can so easily score?

Gateways & Addiction

I'd like to take a moment, if that's okay with you (which it kind of has to be, since I'm writing without you present) to discuss the use of recreational drugs.
And I'm not talking about all drugs in general, but specifically the addictive ones.
And while everything is addictive in modern day life, I mean really addictive.
The ones that will make you want to die without.

Common Misconception: Almost every time, drugs come into people's lives without request.
Drugs are easy to come by. Drugs are easy to take. Drugs are easy to love. Drugs are easy to make sacrifices for.
Drugs do not care. Drugs do not like you as much as you them. Drugs will scar you. When life is not worth living, you are. If you don't want to experience life, try to experience yourself.
Try not to use drugs to distract from who you are.

I have had drug problems throughout life so far. I can imagine I will at some point in the future, that's the nature of them. I lost a friend to heroin two months after I got clean. He was 16 years old, and it was heart breaking. For myself, our friends, and to the family that had shunned him because of his addiction. It's easier to say yes to the plunge of hope, than no to the stillness of refusing. You may want to reach for an escape. There are other escapes. There are less dangerous escapes. There are ways to say no. If you want to try something, I know it is hard to find an alternative, but nine times out of ten they will make you worse. A brief escape is not progression towards fixing a problem.
If you really feel the need to say yes, it's understandable. It happens so much more often than humanity will ever want to admit. make sure you are in the place to say no as well. If you want to try it, make sure it's tasting, not a dependence. But be warned, some addictions sneak so fast than you cannot refuse a second.

As a note to anyone who knows someone reliant on drugs, whether it is a friend or family. You cannot judge. No one asks to be addicted. No one asks to feel the need to take something. One of the most horrific feeling in the world is being judged and despaired at by those closest to you. Just because your life hasn't led you to that problem, it doesn't mean you can't be there for someone who's has.

Don't make it about your feelings towards drugs. Don't judge. Don't neglect.

Do be there. Do ask questions. Do show you care.

16

You should have let me go first, oh brother,
To make sure the Light was safe

Riding

The decision to try heroin was my own, and while it involved a journey I went with on other people, it was my active choice to take that first hit. I still believe, to this day, five days away from being 3 years clean, that I was justified in my choice, and don't think I would have changed that decision was I able to go back. The weight of the world and events in my life at the time were excruciating, and for a short while it was indeed the only thing that could alleviate any of the pressure.

Of course, it very quickly became the problem itself. The first hit I took was after a few months of experimenting with various drugs, ketamine (horse tranquilliser) being the favourite until then. The lack of feeling was what I craved, the spaced skull, the disconnection from my body, the apathy to life. When I was offered an upgrade in the form of a belt and needle it sounded perfect.

The problem with drugs is that they lack perspective.

I was, as most are with heroin, hooked from the first minute.

I don't want to glorify it, but I don't want to lie either.

That first glimpse was like a star illuminating my veins, filling my body with its bountiful light. A gasp that translated to new perspective in life. That moment, the subtle movement of thumbs and my eyes falling to the floor with me, changed my life forever. But heroin is not a love song. It's a bitter, vicious war with no respect or consideration for collateral damage. Heroin is not just strong minded; it is unforgiving and it is relentless.

Let me deter you from temptation by saying life after will be desaturated, grey. It's so hard to find a replacement that brings the same vibrancies to the everyday.

And there was nothing at that time that offered anything like a hit. Life was stressful and ferocious, my mental health felt broken and unrecoverable, and to be honest for a short while I believed drugs kept me alive for a couple of months by taking away to the pain that I would have forcibly removed.

But with heroin comes addiction, and addiction brings a whole new spectrum of discomfort. Discomfort is far too lenient a word for what that lifestyle entails, but it's the only adjective to describe the sensation although it lacks the severity of what the situation entails. In that moment, in that mind set, it's impossible to not crave it.

Living in squalor becomes a choice, an acceptable choice. Sacrifices will be made to anything to Gods that were dealers, nothing could be as important as scraping together money for the hit that would see you through the night. And then pay day's spoils would be emptied instantly in celebration when it came. It all made sense. That was the only way. The only way to happiness. Or synthetic happiness, which was the best I could get.

A few months were wasted this way, day and night spent either in another dimension or sweating for the next release. On a steady diet of cigarettes and smack, my physical health quite obviously deteriorated rapidly. I thought my mental health was the most stable it had ever been. Heroin was almost silencing the voices in my head which was a more than welcome respite, and my agitation seemed justified when sober because I was just craving my next hit. Mania put down as excitement for the next. Depression put down as having to wait for the next. Fury put down as life being cruel that I couldn't afford the next. I t seems logical at the time. But 'the next', was always the problem.

I was incredibly lucky in terms of getting clean. One night while away from sobriety I fell and smashed my elbow, effectively splitting the joint in two. Due to said lack of sobriety, I went to bed and the next morning, drove to work (with one working arm) for an 8-hour shift, struggling to balance a glass in one hand whilst pouring a pint tap with the other. That evening I finally went to hospital, and the following morning had an operation to put a metal plated elbow in. Now due to the morphine and painkillers I was on, I was lucky to escape a couple of days cravings, but after a while they set in. Due to the cast on my arm there was no way to prepare a needle, and I couldn't roll one handed, and couldn't really travel through to my other friends who had similar habits. So, I had to sweat. And writhe. And shout and suffer and curse everything as all my energy was forced into missing chemical release. It's not until after withdrawal has stopped that you release the venomous lies that are held in 'Just one more'. There was no intention of one more. I was furious my entire lifestyle had been stolen from me and I held every intention of going back to full time injecting - I planned to double my efforts.

But there comes a point, not of clarity, but of exhaustion. When the drugs have left your blood and it's only in your head. A point where you have to decide, with the closest thing you'd had to clarity in what feels like a lifetime, what's best for the future, whether you like it or not. It's so much easier to go back. I was so lucky. I could see how I'd affected those around me. Who I'd hurt, and those who I'd snapped at when they had no idea? The people I had cared about, who cared for me. I wasn't at the point where I fully cared for them yet, at least not more than heroin. But I cared enough to admit that they were more important. To go back would be to spit in the faces of everyone who had ever loved me. I didn't want to choose them, but I did. And with that, I began to build.

It takes a while to find a replacement seemingly worthwhile. As I said, life feels grey, like someone lowered the saturation of every experience thereafter to 10%, and with your mind always wandering back to what it might be like to have a taste of that sweetest poison again. It's vital to find something you might one day passionate about. You might not be in the moment. I got almost no enjoyment from playing music when I first got clean, but I built up a new habit. Now 3 years later, it's my new addiction, and one I'm doing things with. Replace and develop. It's a long and agonising process, but it can be treated like the greatest lesson in life. Never judge, never patronise, never choose the easiest option.

Loverboy

Loverboy.
It is 3:17 in the AM
Walls connive and disintegrate
Brick flooding with remnants of your face
Loverboy
Quick with a joke, never without smoke
Winning teeth that distracted from your peeling arm
Loverboy
You grew up on the wrong kind of toy
Never learnt that syringes were not for the Doctors and Nurses
That children might play
But your laugh, swiftly negating curses
No matter what time of day
Loverboy
You are the ghost within my bones
You are the warmth that comforts my soul
You are the blessing of the crass
But all too late it must be accepted,
Loverboy,
That you now belong in the past.

Slope

The slip up.
The mistake that must be let go,
That holds on like a
Cannibal, who has just tasted
his first kiss

Obsession

A permanent need for a particular thing is uncomfortable. To crave something so specific that the mind and body ache and are never able to stop clamoring for, and any sort of contentment is near impossible without finding this release. I loathe the word obsession. It's needy and demanding, it feels impertinent and controlling. But at points you have to admit you hold obsessions over certain things.

Not addictions. This is completely separate issue. It may feel like an addiction at times, but it is impacting in a totally different realm.

And it takes many forms. Activities. Words. Colours. People. It's not nice to obsess over people. For anyone in the area of it. It has made me manipulative and cruel and tiresome, and realistically - a fucking prick. Boundaries need to be set in preparation for this sort of thing. Solid distractions are very much needed.

Part of me wants to argue that some things are okay to obsess over, hobbies, work, that sort of thing: the productive feeling, I suppose. But this really is the opposite of truth. These kinds of obsessions will always lead to disappointment in some way, burnout, for example. It's so important to safeguard yourself from this disappointment because it can absolutely be crippling and emotionally overwhelming.

I once had plans to travel to a city to see someone very close to me and see my favourite band, but due to inclement weather, my bus was cancelled.

I wanted to kill myself. I paced my room tears streaming and voice shrieking for hours on end.

I was able to travel the next day. It was just a delay, but the turmoil it sent me through felt completely unbearable. The strength of those emotions was unparalleled, and frankly, incredibly fucking dangerous.

I couldn't eat, or sleep or sit down, or stop moving, or stop crying, or stop shouting. I truly don't recognise who that person was, or where he came from. I am also aware of how easy it would be for me to become that person again.

I need to keep myself in check. For my own safety and sanity, and to protect those around me that could be impacted by me and my relentless needs. When I feel 'the need' coming on, I quit. Take time off, walk away, leave it alone. I don't want thoughts to control or ruin every aspect of my life, and I can largely see the links of that particular episode with mania, that's exactly why I have to control myself. Because I will lose that control oh so easily. This illness is a relentless power to be reckoned with, a lot of the time my skull feels like it's trapped between an unstoppable force and an immovable object, and I'm being crushed between these titans. So, I have to keep the breathing space there. Never let things get to close that they begin to squeeze or push me. Ensure I always have enough room in anything that I can wiggle out if need be.
It's safer. It's hard, yes. To maybe start something new and have to set time limits on the amount of time I spend on something or hanging out with a friend when it's all I want to do, consistently and repeatedly. It even feels right. But it's not. Reminders are necessary, constant checking, creating imperative limitations.

The hardest part is trying to remain causal about anything exciting.
I find it ironic, really.
The best things can break us.
And break us pretty brutality, too.
Even the absence of obsession can be utterly dominating. The search and the hunger. The unwanted and necessary checking. The itch to find something to crave. Watch it.

Intensity

There is no grey area in the strength of emotions. They are felt fully, to unbound extents for better or for worse. No matter the emotion, the intensity is overwhelming. The slightest levels of joy turn to ecstasy, excitement turns to sheer delight, nerves turn to terror, irritation turns to fury - though my way of processing rage tends to be to just start bawling with tears, it's not an emotion I'm comfortable with in the slightest. Doubt turns to extreme paranoia, upset turns to anguish and depression. And thus, the list goes on. You get the picture.

There isn't really a comfortable middle ground in the emotional spectrum. Everything is felt at 140%. Which in some ways I think is a true blessing - why live life in half measures when you can really feel it to its fullest. The drawbacks are naturally that any negative moods get blown way past any sense of standard proportions. Something as simple as feeling tired can swing rapidly into a bout of exhausting depression, and anxiety can make the entire body freeze.

Mood stabilising medication, which I've trailed in the past, numbs this too much however. It puts life into a little contained box that seems to negate any serious emotion. Which I guess is the whole point, to stop the low moods dipping too low and to ensure that the positive emotions to transpire into becoming mania. However, I found this really intrusive. Mainly as a a writer and a musician who focusses on writing about emotion and self-expression, I no longer felt I was able to express anything. I was clouded to myself, confused about my feelings - or lack of.

So while the intensity of day to day feeling can be overwhelming, I wouldn't really have it any other way. The weight of my feelings might drag me lower than casual emotions should, but they also make me experience life in the most full and blessed way. Joy is elation and angelic - I wouldn't trade that if I can survive the flip side. Which so far, despite myself at times, I have. It's a balance of extremities and learning how to deal with each one. I need to constantly be aware of my needs each minute to avoid any negatively impacting situations and to make sure all the strong feelings are manageable, and as positive as possible.

Unemployment

Statistically only 8% of sufferers of schizophrenia are in employment. I've been unable to distinguish the exact employment rates for schizoaffective disorder, but I imagine they are not too dissimilar. Jobs hold the ability to give people purpose. They also claim the ability to ruin our lives and mental health depending on what we think of them. I've done I loved and adored every shift, working with headphones cleaning dishes in a kitchen, to serving loving locals at a quiet pub, to jobs that have driven me closer than I like to the edge. I think the setbacks that a condition and symptoms of a disorder like this brings tend to make a lot of jobs incredibly difficult - cocktail bars are impossible when you not only have to remember the four different cocktails that party just ordered, but also have to try and recite the recipes of them: out of the 80 cocktails in the menu. Anyone would find this difficult. And to an employer, it's almost understandable not to give that job to someone who struggles to remember things anyway, especially when from the outside perspective the employee is spending most of their time vacantly daydreaming. But this doesn't mean we can't do any job. I've found my relationship to previous work tended to be based on the environment rather than the tasks. I think this is a fair summary when I kept one pub job steady for two years and two weeks in another made me walk onto a bridge where the police pulled me off.
Unemployment is a huge issue, there is no denying it at the present moment. Even if it is slightly more sparse than recent years, it remains a big issue which needs to be tackled.
This is not what this is about.

This is about the other side of employment. The lack of employment. Being unemployed, so to speak. I spent around five months in the unforgiving situation that is living on Great Britain's Universal Credit, where I had to spend '30 hours a week' searching for jobs, despite leaving my previous job due to an attempted overdose. The UK's unemployment program is unforgiving. You also get labelled as 'lazy' and 'scrounging off the system' when really, most of the time, people genuinely have good reasons for being unemployed. I had to go to meetings once every two weeks to ensure I could still have some money to live on. Meetings in a hot, horrendously busy office with people who didn't give two shits about anyone sitting across from them. I had plans to leave Dundee for university which they saw as great, but pressed me to look for jobs I didn't want to do because I clearly wasn't 'that unwell'.

This was the horrible part. I felt too unwell to work or look for jobs, but sitting around doing nothing but focus on voices in my head was equally debilitating. So, I went to the meetings and had a panic attack almost every single time, got sanctioned if I missed one (due to lack of functioning memory), and sat on a laptop staring at websites showing me jobs I was either unqualified to do, or I thought would make me worse. Every month got longer, and I got worse.

Though I also made progress. I had time to sort everything I needed for the future and to try and better myself, which didn't really work. I failed to occupy my time effectively most days, and other days inspiration would hit; inspiration I felt which would never have been found again by being in a job I despised. The cloud over creativity, as I thought of it. I was very fortunate to have an out with starting university, and a lot of people don't have that to look forward to when they're signing on.

I realise I've not offered any solutions here, but if I did have a solution, I'd be screaming it from the streets. I guess I'm just saying that we can work. But it needs to be more understood of when and where we can. And maybe sometimes it needs to be okay not to work. But for fucks sake, we really need a system that treats people like human beings. No one can be reduced to a number. Universal Credit should really try to remember that.

Concentration (or lack thereof)

The reason the chapters in this book is largely born from my severely sporadic concentration level - another common feature in schizoaffective disorder, but also occurs in a trait in several mental health diagnoses. I find it impacting in several, contradictory ways. Primarily is what has affected this piece the most, which is not being able to stare at this keyboard and screen for longer than 20 minutes per session before restlessness and apathy begin to consume my senses. This is incredibly common through my life; in working I need to go between different projects at the same time, in conversation I have a tendency to bounce around topics randomly and rapidly, and in reading I tend to only be able to read one or two pages of a book before either losing interest or getting confused. I think this is why I kept with keeping this format for this - I've often struggled in the past with mental health books that have been thick wads of overflowing words compressed into pages too small to maintain the interest or intrigue of a mind that is permanently seeking something new to focus on. Ideally, the short chapter style of this piece will aid in offering perspective of the mindset I'm trying to explain, or be easier for someone with similar concentration levels to find accessible and progress through. Selfishly, however, it's really to stop myself tearing my hair out over the prospect of huge prolific paragraphs and chapters.

Monetary Abandonment (And Other Charms of Recklessness)

For me, one of most misjudged parts of schizoaffective disorder is the minor tendencies - not to discredit any symptom of an illness, but the ones that are commonly overlooked by a focus on dissociation, hallucination and delusion. There are powerful, but perhaps more everyday trends in the disorder that are often forgotten in general knowledge.
Perhaps most obvious to those that know me, is my inefficiency with money. When people ask me how I was able to afford 73 tattoos' in 4 years - the real answer is idiocy.
I am appalling at maintaining a healthy bank account. Money comes in, and it comes out almost as quickly as the payday transfer has come. The excuses of 'Money is meant to be spent' or my latest moral plea of 'But I'm supporting artists', are really just attempted facades to disguise the fact that I fucking love spending cash. Not necessarily on material objects - tattooing is obviously as exception to this, but I have recently endeavored to take on more of an essentialist approach to the objects I buy, trying to minimise my wardrobe and other purchases. This then leads to me convincing myself that if I'm reducing the quantity of my purchases, I am therefore allowed to increase the quality (and thus value) of what I buy. This has not helped my financial situation develop. Now I just have a bit more space in my drawers.

This is a route of hedonic adaptation that I have not yet been able to quell. This is where we make a purchase, and the new product gives us a rush and thrill, content with whatever item we have acquired and quickly grown to love. Soon, this lust fades, and the product becomes boring to us, so we create rush, another transaction, another fleeting attempt at contentment.

This is my problem with the bank account. When money comes in, there isn't a moment of 'Oh yes, what a good amount of money to see me through the month': the internal dialogue is more along the lines of 'Perfect, I can afford, this, this and this now, and figure out food and bills later'.

Without digressing too much into the details of my debit card, this devil may care attitude to currency has proved a serious downfall in my person. Debt, missed events and disappointment have all been the result of my short-lived excitement at the prospect of a number. A fucking number and tapping 4 digits in to a machine. It shouldn't be thrilling - but it often is for those of my condition. Of course, perhaps it could be argued that this trait is a fault of my own foolishness, and perhaps using a diagnosis as a scapegoat for blame; maybe even an excuse to continue the habit.

Maybe. I'll work on it.

Other symptoms that tend to hold a lack of realisation include the deprivation and difficulty of physical movement, and inherent lack of emotion in the face and speech. I find my physicality to be affected in two main ways - largely dependent on mood and/or the type of episode I might be experiencing. During mania or what I self-label a 'deranged and hopeless psychosis', my movement is frenzied. I may attempt to keep myself still which leads to shaking, and can only be held for so long before lashing in outbursts - not meaning to be violent, but sheer agitation may make them to appear so. This can include real violent outbursts directed at myself or inanimate objects (I have wreaked havoc upon bedrooms many a time whilst being unable to stop my body charging) or continual pacing and shaking for hours on end - probably a more comfortable sight for an onlooker than the former, but a time filled with relentless dread and stress. In other episodes that center more around depression, moving becomes almost impossible. At a time, for two days straight I never ventured further than my hands and knees, only crawling to the toilet and back to bed - each trip taking around 20 minutes to cover the 9ft trek. It can enforce hours or days in isolation, curled upon the floor in desperation.

More often than I care to admit - I have to put real effort into displaying emotion. Without wanting to seem rude to a conversational companion, I've had to practice 'polite chatter'. Most of the time I'm good at it - in fact, I find other people fascinating, and want nothing more to emotionally engage with everyone I meet. At times however, I struggle. I feel my eyes, face and voice become void of meaning or care, and it seems an impossible task to put effort into displaying affection. It's like a state of obtuse nonchalance, or a lasting wave of apathy - or so it comes across. Similarly, it can happen during my own speaking, particularly if talking about myself or my troubles. Like an emotional detachment. A form of dissociation, perhaps.

As I mentioned before, this is not a work on the scientific exploration of schizoaffective disorder, merely a documentation and highlighting of my experiences of suffering the affliction. If you're looking for a full list of symptoms and explanation, please look elsewhere, for there are far more than I wish to cover here. The main other things that have had prolific impacts on my person are challenged, at times, with memory, speech; diction, forming sentences (coming on from confused or disorganised thought patterns), stammering etc., and severe lack of motivation. It becomes so easy to live inside your head when it feels like a cage.

The Reality of Hallucinating

Many people have heard the term hallucination, many have an idea of what that entails, and some may even have tried to imagine such an experience. Sadly, sensory hallucination is something which can never be deeply understood until it has been experienced - and even then, not always. They can affect every sense, and are rarely anything that could be expected. The term schizophrenia comes with certain weight and a seeming definition, perhaps a stereotype that can be assumed, and easy to assume what the experienced hallucinations might be. However, they stretch much further than having voices in the head that do not exist, and more terrifying than moving shadows and lights. They can happen anywhere, anytime - naturally stress can cause acute episodes to be more severe and frequent, but psychosis can take place constantly over long periods of time too.

This has been my experience with voices. I have heard them consistently since the age of 12: and since then I fail to recall a moment where they have not been present. There are hundreds - most of whom are people I know. I feel as though if I hear someone speak once in my life, their voice is forever embedded in my cortex. At times they whisper and mutter amongst each other, others they shriek and rage directly at me. They never speak kindly, only the most derogatory language suits their vocabulary. They know my fears, my anxieties, my phobia's and they use them well against me. I am forced to worry about things I know I should not, doubt casted into the most secure areas of my life.

They order my mouth shut when I try to open to people, they ruin my trust with those around me, I have to fight every morning to just get out of bed. Or eat. Or see friends. Or read. Or write this.

I find it ironic that they hate me so. Without me they would have no home. They exist through me, and despise me. Maybe they hate their own existence, and blame me for it. Maybe they don't want me to kill myself. They just want to die with me as soon as possible.

They plague insults into my skull, pushing me to believe obvious lies about myself, never contented. They are never content. As much as I might work on my weight or push my productivity until I exhaust my very soul - it is not enough. They feed on my lack, on my limits. They feed on every thought that is my own.

There are different types of voices. External and internal. These that I have described are the internal, the ones that I am able to confine within my brain and label hallucinations. They are severe and they are pestilence, but I can locate them within myself. They live in the lumps on the back of my skull, where I hear them constantly. And when I tire or can no longer ignore them, they blitzkrieg forward. I feel the noise and their presence wash forward from the base of my skull to the top, like an itch that would need a hammer to get rid of. In my worst episodes they come forward still, to the tip of my hairline. No amount of massaging or compulsive clutching can rid them from here, they have made ground and intend to keep it. And worse still, in the worst acute moments, the come lower. When I am at my worst, I feel the voices sit in the back of my eyes, I hear their screams from here. It is blinding and deafening. I can still see but notice nothing - there is no connection to the outside world; my pupils become cages to world I cannot reach. And these are the worst of them all. When voices alone have negated my other senses, trapped me in my mind with them, like starving wolves playing with their kill.

External voices are more confusing for me, and maybe don't match to the same venomous evil of the internal ones, but make up for it with disarray and a sense of loss. They create new conversations in my head - misremembrance and falsities are scattered across my brain. They link closely with delusion. Trying to find the radio planted in the walls. The man on the News informing me that the world will end if I don't cut myself. It's the news. Why would I not believe it? These kinds are not always obvious hallucinations - in fact, they very rarely are. They adapt real situations, film and TV's may have very different lines to the normal version, the person behind you in the pub is bitching about you and knows all of your secrets, the book is a call to arms. These voices bring delusion. Because I am unaware of their origin until later (sometimes much later, sometimes never) I find it very difficult to believe these things are not true.

These can become, daily, the real controllers, the catalysts of self-destruction, or the origin of confusion and upset.

And this is just the work of the voices.

The other senses can become even more drastic.

Visual Hallucinations can be vastly different, on a spectrum of theme, severity and impact. They can be triggering, disrupting, disarming and intoxication. And I am not describing flashing images in the mind, I'm talking about seeing, through the same eyes as anyone else, things that others do not. Because we generally believe our eyes do not deceive, they are impossible not to be convinced by in their reality. One of worst episodes involved hours locked in my room, believing my rapist was on the other side, and calling the police.

I think the easiest way to transcribe their effects is to detail my most common visuals.

The Waves: The waves are glimmering shifts of light, like ripples of colours that skitter across walls and floors in obvious directions. They lead somewhere. I don't know where - I've never reached the end of where they try to take me. I once spent five hours wandering through the streets and alleys of Manchester trying to track down the source of these incandescent navigators, but gradually grew tired - and very lost. They seem to evoke an urge, a necessity, that demands to be followed. I experience them randomly, maybe as frequent as twice per month, but they command complete attention. All other activities must be dropped to begin pursuit. When they appear, an animalistic urge takes hold of me - I must answer whatever call this is. They ultimately end in depressive states, as eventually the waves stop suddenly and I can no longer find them, or I realise what I'm doing: chasing imaginary lights. This is both disappointing for never reaching their crux, and for repeatedly giving into the pleasure of whatever journey I feel embark on, despite the awareness of it's delusional origin.

Mirrors: Mirrors always play on insecurities. They hide nothing, and so we see nothing we like. We look at the insecurities that we spend the rest of our days trying not to think about. They also play tricks. They do not move when I do, and vice versa. I brush my teeth and watch myself take a blade to my throat. Thousands of spiders sprinting and covering my body while I do my hair. Spending hours trying to wash blood and spunk off of my neck. I see myself as a child. I see myself with my mouth stitched shut. These are daily horrors. I often wonder if I even know what I look like. In recovery, I have learned it is best for me to avoid mirrors. I used to use them near constantly, narcissism demanding I look for my reflection in every shop window. I have minimised my use. They terrify my eyes; I never know what I might see. It's like the world's shittiest lottery. Maybe I'm scared I'll actually see a true reflection. Right now, I don't know what concept I find more terrifying.

Blood, Ropes, Numbers: There is blood and oil on the walls of rooms. There are nooses that dangle from the ceilings. There are numbers (4,23,64,361) that have no explanation and I cannot figure out. These are sporadic, they are random, they are sudden. I feel as though I am sensing the rooms past, but it does not happen every time I go into the room. Any room, some of the time. These have become the least threatening of my hallucinations. They are no longer surprising and bring only a low shudder to my pine. You grow accustomed to some, especially in comparison to the horror-show of others.

Benjamin: I've been without Benjamin only a handful of times in the past 8 years. I don't remember when he came to me, and I don't recall life without his presence easily. At least, I can't recall what it's like not to feel his presence. He doesn't like nicknames. I assume, he doesn't speak. He's tall, over 6ft, but he slumps and has few visible features. He wears a black cloak from head to toe, chains around his wrists and his ankles. The clink. Constantly. Other than this he makes no sound. His face is shrouded in the shadows of his hood, but long, black hair of silk swings gently as he walks. His cloak is torn and tattered, his chains rusted, his bare feet black with oil. For a while I believed the obsidian on his bare skin was like a tattoo, but I've realised its oil that covers his limbs. It drips from him occasionally. I can smell it. He carries with him a box of matches in his left hand, always. He's never lit one. I guess it would bring self-immolation, and he knows it. I believe he is intelligent. He usually just watches, and follows, every movement I make. When I walk down the street he follows slowly behind, and then is around the corner waiting for me. He stands against the wall and watches me read. He sits across from me when I masturbate (leading to a lack of). His eyes, though I cannot see them, are heavy and perceptive and above all, focussed. It's as if he is waiting for something. He comes close when the voices get loud, he stands over me and reaches his hand out. Not to touch me, I used to think that was his intention, but no, he's like a conductor that brings the other tongues to crescendo. I feel he is their spy; he watches my mistakes in the day and observes my anxieties, and later confers with the others in my skull so they have educated targeting against me. I don't think he is evil. He is merely cold. His presence is thus - not of malicious intent or a negative inclination, merely a frozen aura of longing that surrounds his steely posture. He never goes. He never speaks. He never moves unless driven by inherent purpose. He likes corners and doorways. He reeks of petroleum and cheap red wine.

I don't know who he is or anything of his origin. I just know him as Benjamin. I named him as a young teenager, and he didn't seem disagreeable. He's never seemed anything. Only present.

As mentioned previously, hallucinations can afflict all of the senses, such as Benjamin having a smell that I perceive clearly. Sometimes I can feel the touch of things that are not there also. Like handcuffs at my wrists or a hand around my throat. The pressure of a ghost chastising my physical embodiment. Perhaps they hold me in envy. Thankfully, this is not so common. I think a more accessible example of this could be sleep paralysis - which has been theorised to be a form of psychosis. Or perhaps Incubi are real, and sleep paralysis is a deeper evil.
I could believe that.
I think I do believe that.

Sorry.
I'm off topic.

Memory

One thing often overlooked as a symptom with schizoaffective disorder is the lack of clarity that comes with memory. Naturally it is confusing and perplexing when the past is mixed with hallucinations and blips from when voices were rife, but everyday remembrance is also a forgotten issue. Dates and times become omitted or muddled together, the company we keep in events seems guiltily replaceable. I often remember the conversations, but not my partner in the words we spoke. I usually remember the time and the place but the face becomes blurred and irretrievable.

It's a horrid thing, one that inspires guilt, to forget the presence of a friend in any situation, or for important things you have been told to slip from your minds grasp. Forgetting the face and the voice, becomes a heart-breaking experience. Events lose their potency when you can't recall who you shared them with.

The other problem them with this is the everyday need for memory. I actually wrote this chapter twice in some twisted irony before realising, months later and abroad, I had done it already.

I'm generally able to remember important events coming up or things I need to do, but a lot of time things go missing from my mind, so I've developed a system that tries to jog my memory when it's failing. I tend to write everything in a notepad, everything. I use different notepads for different things, one as a journal where I can bullet point daily to do lists, summarise events in a week, month and each day, and write short reviews at the end of each day including detailed notations of where I've been and with who, what I was doing, so I can look back and keep everyday life in mind.

I use a different book for phrases or words, as a lyricist/poet I try to note down every single idea that pops into my head, usually consisting of anywhere between 2 words and 2 sentences. If I didn't note these smaller ideas now, I'd never finish anything. A lot of the time I find myself struggling on how to progress or to develop ideas on a piece; this helps me find similar phrases that might work, or even fit perfectly, that are long forgotten to my conscious.

I sleep next to sticky notes and a pen in case memories or ideas appear in the night and write them down before they go. I cover my room in the sticky notes, the wall dependent on what the content is; task, idea, what I did last month, shopping list. These are always kept in easy view when in my room; tasks put in hierarchy next to the door, with the most important things on the door itself. If it's something I need to do outside, I take a photo of what's on the door and frequently check it when I'm out. It's no use having a system to remind you of everything in your room if it fails in the 8 hours, you're not in it.

It takes a while to figure out. It's all practice and repetition through frustration and tediousness.

III

The Outside

To Those It Does Not Concern: Stop talking about other people's weight.

A Monologue to Assumptions

In 60 seconds, faces are shown
In 60 seconds, minds are not blown
But judgements become created
And those thoughts become animated,
I've been here almost a minute
We have no plan so by teeth we'll skin it
And I'll show how your lies are not mine
And that you are wrong more than half the time,
60 seconds.
What do you see?
Peroxide, fake blonde hair,
A glazed vacant stare
Where is he from?
A Jock you may mock in the street
Do you wonder if he has tattoos on his feet?
Judgements will put him through stress
And he's a singer you never want to see shirtless,
Abused, broken, volatile, dull
These words plaster across his face
Your mouth, your eyes, your lips conjoin
Your judgements echo like the Battle of the Boyne,
Has he got tattoos to cover his track marks?
Must be a junkie, might be high, says he's clean?
That's a lie,
But your judgements never stop to wonder why
Abused by a man when he was boy,
Every action has its equal reaction,
Every judgement has a resulting consequence,
Every person has a fucking story.

Breaking Stigma

Judgements and stigma still seem to reside prominently in modern life, particularly around topics such as mental health, trauma, addiction and recovery. Everyone loves a good recovery story - but most don't like to dwell on the details involved. Or seem to be aware of the struggles of other people, unable to thus far fulfil their recovery story. When society is haunted by invisible taboos it makes silence grow in those unfortunate souls experiencing problems. We live in a world where everything outside a traditional status quo must be admitted to, as if difference is something that has to be explained. We 'admit' to our problems in such a reluctant manner due to the fact that the world has conditioned us to feel shame. We are told to be successful, driven, happy, slim but not too slim, wealthy, not in debt, to follow every ounce of legality (until you're of a high enough societal standing to ignore a few laws without much notice) and above all, to keep things to ourselves. If we can't match these criteria, we are indoctrinated to believe in ourselves as failures - but who can do all of these things?

Life does not begin on an even playing field. Everyone born into different lifestyles, opportunities and futures. It's so damaging to focus our life goals upon the privileged few who are designed to build dissatisfaction in our lives in an effort for us to consume more products that will improve ourselves.

Stigma is still very much rife in our world. We see it every day in a huge variety of forms. Things are certainly improving - depression & anxiety have a much more widespread conversation, along with many other mental illnesses becoming much more well known about. I however, feel this is largely lacking around schizophrenia, psychosis and their counterparts. After mentioning it to my diagnosis to people, they tend to assume a Hollywood portrayal of serial killers or that they are in the presence of a psychopath. Both definitions are far from accurate - schizophrenia/affective disorder is one of the most misinterpreted, badly portrayed, and lesser known of mental health conditions. People seem to find the concept scary - which it of course is, experiencing psychosis is naturally terrifying. However, it seems to me that people assume the illness is externally violent, that I may be branded as dangerous and aggressive, but this is not true. People living with schizophrenia are, in most cases, far more likely to be victim of aggressive behaviour than the perpetrator, and it is incredibly likely that they would only inflict hurt upon themselves, not someone else. This has been my experience. I have never wanted to wish harm to another person due to my illness, nor been instructed to hurt anyone. Psychosis for me, is always directed internally.

There are of course exceptions, but as are there with, quite literally, anything. Labels have become an incredibly dangerous weapon, which goes unrealised by most. Words bare weight and can bring pain - terminology should not be thrown around lightly. We need to be aware of the language we use and more importantly why we use it - any word whose intention is born from judgement or degradation should not be used, and should not be used as freely as we see every day. Every time someone is called 'psycho', 'mental', or 'crazy' without cause (or even if), it enforces a label onto someone, and this leads to engraving stigma on a group. Diagnosis are just diagnosis - and should be viewed as this. There is reason why a term on a medical form should make an individual any less than their peers.

When we can remove the stigma from these words, these names, we can remove the shame from them too. Think, adapt and select the language we use to bring a more positive future. I'm disgusted the term 'Loony Bin' still exists. And still conveys the same imagery as it did when it was coined at the end of the 18th century. Surely, we should have adapted our dialect by now? The evolution of science has brought with it evidence that there are no such thing as 'lunatics': there is only mental illness. And just like illness of the body, we should treat this with care and compassion, not ridicule and spite.

It is vital all stigma surrounding mental health is broken, if we are to grow as a supportive and caring society - and why would anyone not wish for that? Every person who tells their story, shares their experience, or nods in agreement to someone else's tale, is doing something towards this movement. Shame must be eradicated for the good of so many people. Share everything. Have no fear of judgement. 'The Norm' is born from enough people creating a movement that sets in place. Anyone can aid this movement. Make shamelessness the norm. Abolish ignorance. This is a movement that can take place anywhere. With friends in the pub. In a book shop by yourself. On social media, broadcasting to the world. Spread awareness and we spread acceptance.

Schizophrenia, and mental illness as a hole is nothing to be ashamed of, nor dangerous.
Stigma is.
We must never judge for experiences different to our own.

Things That Need to be Normalised

Having conversations with food.
Talking to yourself. However incessantly it might be.
Showering 4 times a day when stressed.
Highlighting and taking notes in books.
Crying due to imaginary scenario's that never happen.
Eating raw mushrooms when upset. Or happy. Or anytime.
Not talking about people's weight or diet.
Not liking the hours of 5pm to 8pm.
Being honest about thoughts & feelings.
Not being 'okay'. Nobody even knows what 'okay' is anyway.

Something to Remember, Always (II)

Self-worth and self-esteem are not linked.
Self-esteem is how you feel about yourself and it is okay for that
to be shit (to an extent), but self-worth is how you'll let other
people treat you, and that is always something to be aware of.
Even when your Self-Esteem is at its lowest, do not let your Self
Worth crumble, because the world is filled with vultures who
will watch you erode and use what remains.

Purgatory

For the past several weeks I have been tormented with a belief, batting one side of rationally I cannot be right and am therefore delusional, and wagering that my gut is correct. This past week I have decided my gut is correct.

I am already dead.

It explains a lot. Why doctors will not help, why I'm failing to connect with other people no matter how much I reach out, why all joy ends moments after it is felt, why nothing is progressing except time. Everything is staying the same, only the minutes change.

This realisation brings mixed feelings of relief and hopelessness. When this doesn't exist, it's comforting to know that nothing really matters and ultimately affects nothing. Though this means suffering has no point and has no escape.
I have plateaued.
My mental health is no longer degrading, but is no longer rising. Not having an episode gives me anxiety of when the next bout will arrive, and it feels worse when it is there as I feel I should have been more prepared. I do not believe in other people. I fail to believe in myself.
I find joy in specific moments and depression in the age that separates each one.

If I am dead, I must regain life and bring it here.
And if I cannot, then this what it means to be self-aware and unable to change.
If life is hell, living is purgatory. Hating the breathing moments and the menial tasks obligation demands in the name of 'life', but not knowing how to change the course. I have tried. I have tried for Heaven and for Hell.

Everything is pending. Waiting, always. For someone to reply. For a doctor referral. For food to cook. For a new film to come out. For happiness. Patience is required for this never-changing reality where everything 'takes time' while nothing progresses. Patience in patients is required. But patient's requirements are never met.

I don't even know what I'm waiting for anymore.

Marketing

Western Society, as whole, is being sold stigma. From the films
we watch, to the adverts forced into our eyes, to the language
used in newspapers - we are being told to doubt ourselves, and
unknowingly yet willingly buy it. Articles using words 'psycho'
to describe people that need help, reports of celebrities 'Coming
Out' with an admittance of mental health problems. We should
celebrate admittance and never label it as something like this;
this has planted an idea that it is something that you have to
admit, and should hide until you're ready to tell people. Of
course, this is an option, but so is openness and honest - every
celebrity that has to come out about a mental health problem
reinforces the idea that it is not the norm. Yes, the conversation
around mental health is vastly expanding and rightly so, but the
wrong language is being used.

The problems, sadly, do not stop here. By using photo shopped
images of 'perfect people' to market clothes and in our films,
we are sold unrealistic standards of the 'right' way to look.
There is no right way to look: otherwise evolution would made
us all look like that. Retail Manufacturers are (somehow legally)
able to sell images to make us hate ourselves, and then make
more money by selling us way to 'correct' our bodies. This is a
dangerous, dangerous game. Unattainable standards lead to
crippled self-esteem and seriously harm people. These industries
are led by closed minded arbiters who believe they can dictate
what beauty is in the name of making money No one can define
beauty. It's subjective, on a spectrum, and arrogant to assume
someone has the right who is beautiful and who is not.

All humans are.

That is the human experience.

We have evolved into what we are now; a variety of beautiful
shapes and sizes, for a reason, and we are to be told we are
wrong and must correct ourselves.

Corporations have no right to play God. They have no right to
hurt people. To damage people. To not be diverse. To advertise
in falsities.

No one has that right - but everyone has the responsibility to be against it.

In film and tv we see similar circumstances; the world's most attractive men and women displayed on our screens conveying whatever story the script permits; but we still see type-cast archetypes of what each character should be represented by. We all have an image of leading man. A leading woman. A funny supporting role. These all provide us with images in our head because we're so used to the same 'look' playing the same roles. There is such little diversity.
How can we accept ourselves for being different when we never see anyone who is different? Not to mention the budgets of filmed media that set the standards higher with perfect lighting and make-up in every shot. There is no realism.

It's so vital to never look to closely into the various media platforms that we are bombarded by. It is in no way conducive to a healthy lifestyle or mental state. Celebrate differences. No human can decide what should or not be okay. We can only accept that we don't look like the products of billion-dollar industries. And I really do believe that's okay.

Meaning

It has occurred to me, and many others, life seems to be a meaningless journey through turmoil and triumph resulting in an inevitable demise. We are killing our planet, killing each other in war and inequality, unjustified crime goes unpunished and any sort of movement that might aid our planet and society is mocked.
A massive fraction of the population is depressed and a terrifyingly high amount of lives end in suicide, science plunders on and religions claim a higher cause, but no one is any closer to finding out why we are here, what for, and if we matter.

These are terrifying thoughts to the depressed or unstable mind.

If life is meaningless then maybe so is suicide. So is suffering. So are content relationships and that watch you spent a huge amount of savings on just to look a bit flash to impress other people that don't matter.
These questions and concepts are not healthy.
I am guilty of contemplating life outside of my life, but there is no use.
There is only worry in that, never joy.
The present is the only place you will ever find happiness. Life outside of the moment you are living is meaningless; the past cannot be changed, the future does not exist, and anything outside of your own experience will only ever be a consideration, not a certainty. Maybe there is a comfort in that. A comfort in purgatory. A comfort in a chaotic world and a ruined life. If it doesn't matter, you can only focus on what you experience in your own moments of consciousness. Life will hurt and it will scar, but there will be times, perhaps the briefest of times, but those moments will matter to you. And that will always be more important than the things that are meaningless.

Everything will be experienced. Pain will fade and joy will come with contentment, contentment of all the experiences of life. And if you can't stop focusing on the lack of meaning, there is a dark comfort: We all die eventually. Might as well see what happens in life before it happens.

Descent

Burn it down,
The mirage matters not
This charade earns no focus
No spotlight should shine on this plain
It screams and shakes that we do not give it
What it claims to deserve
When it kills and maims
Drives mad all who enter
Which is, everyone.
Burn it down,
Take all that is not real from my eyes
Leave me blind
Such a pain would not exist
Anywhere else but in Hell
Inconceivable,
For a soul to exist in a realm
Which he refutes the presence of,

Protecting the Mental Health of the Youth

This may actually be a slightly misleading title, as what I want
to say applies to everyone, of all generations. However, I think
it is important to stress the importance of taking action to aid
younger people in the modern world right now, with mental
illness statistically growing, and I'm a firm believer that the
voice of the youth is more resonant than it ever has been before.
Whether you agree or disagree with my slagging off of modern
society so far in this book, I don't think there's any hiding from
the fact that at the moment, we know far more and far less about
mental illness than we have done in human history. Sadly, it is
an arbitrary fact that mental health is also more widespread and
common than ever, almost definitely down to our ever-
increasing knowledge on the subject and ability to diagnose the
specific problems, instead of hospitalising people and saying
they are 'not themselves'. However due to the increasing
epidemic of mental health problems, I have already argued this
is down to the way modern life is run, and furthermore, perhaps
it's more shocking to be someone who isn't suffering some sort
of issue beneath their skulls with the relentless pressure of
modern life and all of its many institutions.
So, how do can help the younger generations on our planet to
develop healthy mind sets under the constant friction of social
life. Is this even an endeavor we can effectively undertake? Or
are we already so far gone on building on negative foundations
that the towers of mind-pollution are going to negate the healthy
progress of anyone from this point forward?
I truly, truly hope not.
Which leads to the question of what can we actually do to shield
the shit from those we love.
With luck, hope and empathy, hopefully a fair bit. And of
course, I don't mean these points to be encouraged to only the
youth of the world, I think these are things we can all learn from
and take forward in consideration to collectively build a
healthier society, and world.

1. Learn openness. Teach openness. No matter what the circumstance, age, class, gender, sexuality, race, whether you have a Tesco Club card, if you shop in Waitrose, if you read poetry every night or spend every weekend on a three-day bender off your face; learn and teach openness. This is a consistent, never ending endeavor. We as a species need to learn to be open with each other, lovers, families, friends, strangers. We've lost all sense of trust in what we do not know - our ancestors were all kin together; they cared and loved every member of their tribe no matter how many people that counted up to. How many people do you love now? Do you permit yourself to feel love for strangers? If we can't all care about each other, then we become open to world that wants to abuse one another. We need to accept our differences and stop harassing each other online or in person for them. We need to help the people we see need help. If someone is crying down the middle of the street, it's now common to walk past them without looking. Worse than this, it's outlandish to ask if a stranger is okay, even if they are evidently not. How is this conducive to a healthy human race? We've lost all empathy towards anyone except a select few. Our new tribes. Because we sacrificed our old ones to build a new world, and in the new world came division. A division that is more prominent than ever, and is forever neglecting mental health. One quarter of the population suffers mental health problems at some point in life. And yet if we see a stranger suffering, we do nothing. What if everyone did that to everyone? If we just ignored a quarter of the entire population? If we assume that the person crying on the street has someone to talk to and is therefore none of our business, what happens when they don't have anyone? How are we not torn inside, every day, by seeing other people's problems and do nothing? Being able to help is of course circumstantial on both sides, but we can do other things. We can speak openly about the shamelessness of mental health and its problems; we can remove degrading or vicious words from our vocabulary so the schizophrenic at the pub doesn't hear someone being called 'psycho' for losing their temper. We can encourage those around us to speak. Ask someone, really ask someone in your

life how they are. Mean the question, evoke the answer. We must consistently and boldly break down the walls held around so called 'taboo' subjects in order for us to heal, as a whole. As a tribe. We must accept everything about each other without judgement and without hate. Every judgement has consequences. If a parent constantly degrades other people for their weight, the child will definitely notice that. They will definitely become increasingly aware of it and it could lead to serious problems later in life. Tiny changes make huge differences. But tiny changes must be made. We must heal as a collective.

Social media is the greatest blessing and the mightiest plague to have dawned upon us in the 21st Century. I've already made my views on it very clear, so I'll do my best not to repeat myself.

Comparison and competition create collusion and internal chaos. Social media was never intended to become a pedestal of ego or a stream 'Look how great my life is', but that is sadly what it has become. It has beautiful opportunities, to show people around the world and their lives, to keep up to date with your favourite bands, to see what long lost friends are up to, and to share the valued parts of your own paths. But we must limit our use somewhere. The dangers must be learned early, and the friction to swerve off addictions implemented swiftly. It's too easy to get lost in the world of followers and likes and super models and fashion we can't afford and why is Brian buying a house at 21 and I've just started uni and look how great Gemma looks scuba diving in the Caribbean while I gorge myself on crisps and hummus. It's okay to gorge on crisps and hummus sometimes. It's never okay to envy someone else's life - particularly when the screenshots of that life have been carefully selected for the highlight reel of 'online presence'. We must remember that no one ever shares the full story online. We must learn not to follow everything we need to - we don't. If reading political tweets every day upsets and frustrates you every day, you don't have to read them. There is no obligation to follow particular things, or to use social media at all. Of course, it does have its positives, hugely so. And it's perfectly possible to narrow our usage down to those positives. But it's equally easy to slip out of them. Teach wariness. Learn wariness. The internet is too vast for us not to sucked into without discipline. Discipline must be kept.

The things most vital to the succession of the progression in the healing process, or the development of our ability to cope with mental illness - or any stress, for that matter - comes from being able to build healthy habits that we can use routinely. I've already spoken about what exactly this might entail, but I haven't resonated enough the importance of encouraging those around us to the same. We see examples of people silently calling for help every single day; alcoholism in younger generation seems to be accepted as a normality for the students who spend every single day in the pub to escape their stress, and other than that, if you smoke cannabis every day and it's your biggest comfort, you may well be addicted. So maybe it's about setting examples to those we can see unhealthy trends in - obviously without overstepping our boundaries, and in a way that doesn't come across as condescending, we can offer a little helping hand to anyone around us who may need it. If someone speaks to you about wanting to go the gym, offer to take them. Maybe there's an anxiety that stops them. Offer to cook a friend a hearty meal. Show people healthy habits without being patronising, lead by example, show empathy and care. It shouldn't be so hard to look after one another. Really, we just should.

Unsocial Media

The everlasting decay of the most popular displeasure in modern society, unbelievably, isn't great for Mental Health. In anybody. Who would have thought a plethora of comparison, distasteful opinions, body shaming, segregating humor and filtered-out-flaws-to-conceal-imperfection could possibly be a detriment to us?

In Matt Haig's book, Notes On A Nervous Planet (read it, love it, incinerate your internet router), he talks about how modern life is almost designed to stress us out, through hedonic adaption and other social elements (read it, love it, I don't want to explain the whole thing), but also talks in detail about our lack of appreciation for what is outside of our lives. We share everything, and when scrolling for hours on end (also known as a thumb workout), we see what everyone else has shared. We process far too much about things that do not affect us. When was the last time you looked out a window for longer than a glance? You might notice something new. When was the last time you stood on grass, and not just walked over it? Your feet will thank you. Screens that we feast on for content might show what life is for others, but you need to be aware of your own.

Social media for the unwell is dangerous. People can be mirages of themselves, and you begin to compare yourself to a perfectly falsified photograph. People can also be horrible. Meme's and jokes and outright insults can be upsetting to read - nothing is not joked about online.

Limiting my use of social media was inspiring. I focus on the folk in my life rather than the faces that live in a 6-inch screen. I'm far more productive - time once wasted by my thumb workouts is now used for reading, exercising or really watching a film. As in actually watching it, noticing everything. Not just glancing to the background noise it's creating while I'm on Twitter. The initial cost feels strange, am I missing out on anything?

The answer, simply, is no. I still go on the usual platforms once a day, and I post to Instagram regularly - but the decision was to ensure I was posting for my own benefit (memories, marketing, the occasional moment I don't think I look like a goblin), but I know it's for me to look back on, and not get bogged down into likes and comments.

It can be nice.

But you need to make it so.

Rules for Unsocial Media

- Start by trying a detox between one week and one month
- Unfollow everyone that provides anything less than a satisfactory reaction
- Turn off all notifications for likes/comments etc
- Post whatever you want
- Put all Social Media Apps in a folder together (maybe even put on password on the folder, just to be a nuisance)
- Do something you've wanted to do for ages (start photography, drawing, relight your passion for Humphrey Bogart films)
- It's a highlight reel of the best of lives, people never show themselves truthfully (It's like a CV for your personality)
- Let go. It will be weird - which is the weird part. Remember life before the like button and statuses. Remember going to the pub and not Snap-chatting the whole thing. Remember you've never needed it.
- Remember real life will always give you more value.

Encouragement

Surrounded
By glinting eyes and raised brows
Now, stand grounded
Experiences brought into reality
A daisy
Petals wilt but the stem grows
Reaching and climbing and growing yet dying
Resistance to be stepped
Resistance to be ignored
Resistance in living, craving to be adored

Walk further
Faces turn towards erosion
Smiles turn towards the wilting
Eyes gleam upon what petals there are left
Words of praise exclaim and connive
Exploiting a beauty which features toxicity
Encouragement that is blind for the ears to see
For the mind to feel
For the body to touch
The first glimpse, the first rush
The first words of contentment are never enough
The daisy blooms, sheds its skin
Revealing the pale rose, resting within
All eyes bewildered with admiration and astonishment
Encouraging the new found beauty towards contentment

But the first words remain
The words that should not have been said
The motivation for the hunger
That fills hospital beds.
They proclaim love for the first
For the rose as if it were the last
But soon they also wilt
Unable to forget it's past

So, the rose must shed more
Until the rest are pleased
Hunger for those first looks
That brought weakness to their knees

But those petals keep falling
As hungry eyes despair
They see not what they have done
For Regret requires care
So, the hunger is increased
And the Roses hunger is noticed
She screams back her resistance
But their attention has deceased.

Suicide in Humor

Is joking about suicide a coping mechanism or disrespectful? In the modern age, jokes involving suicide or mental health have become frequent, particularly within mental health communities. There used to be a theory that behind every dark joke was a blatant truth, a cry for help. I would argue that now, however, this has become confused with the desensitisation of mental health, self-harm, and suicide. Within minutes of use of social media, we can see the signs that mental health has become a bit of a meme, perhaps even a trend, and that the language involved has become incredibly misused. People often describe themselves as 'A bit OCD' or 'God I'm so Bipolar', or perhaps go as far as to tweet 'Got work in an hour, maybe I'll just kill myself'. Not only are these jokes inaccurate, they become degrading generalisation. And whilst I'm not negating these jokes come from somewhere, and very likely do give glimpses that need to be addressed. Maybe we've become too lenient with our language in humor and in how we approach discussions of suicide. We need to remember these words hold incredibly serious issues and perhaps should not be used so frivolously.

Each joke, especially when broadcast as publicly as on social media, could be a potential trigger for any other user. I'm a firm believer we have a responsibility to the other people that we share our words with - a responsibility to not take risks on hurting or upsetting someone for the sake of a joke. And while the line 'it was just a joke' might seem an easy and somewhat justifiable excuse, but jokes have always been in the name of causing laughter, not distress.

Language is not menial; this cannot be denied. Being wary is a shared responsibility, that we never rub salt in someone's unnoticed wound. The lack of personality in social media has pushed us to forget our sense of humanity - with everyone only displaying the highlights reel of their lives and scrolling past words that have lost all meaning, it's easy to see how we can forget the other eyes reading the screens on the flip side. This is worsened still by how quickly things are able to trend on social media; one share of a joke can lead to thousands, and the original perpetrator becomes faceless to their audience so that only the joke exists, and no human face is registered with it. This makes it easier to make these jokes since we can hide behind screens and IP addresses, not think about the fact other humans will register these words in some way. Any human online can see anything, and be affected in any way. We are human. Let us please remember we have humanity, and it is precious.

We need to remember the loosening of our own vocabulary when we are in bad ways. It's easy to slip into making these jokes ourselves, to forget that these words may burn those who care for us. They hear none of the fake laughter, only the desperation and intent behind each syllable. This humor can haunt them. Be wary.

The Bastards

The media makes people doubt themselves and demonise themselves with advertised self-consciousness in a never ending, countless, 'death by a thousand cuts' sort of way. It sells unattainable (literally, via photo editing and million-dollar shoots) standards of beauty as the norm - combined with magazines and newspapers shaming any celebrity with the slightest 'imperfection' in photographs. There is no imperfection with the human body. There is no way it is 'supposed' to look, apart from like a human body.

The danger of selling falsified looks is obvious - people compare themselves to it and see themselves as ugly, causing self-doubt, self-loathing, and self-destruction.
The power of photographs and words has been forgotten in the modern day. Social media, and all media, has stripped us of the intimacy and sentimentality of what a photograph means. Now, they are a means for 'beautiful' people to indulge and advertise, and for 'lesser' people to compare themselves, lose confidence themselves, and at worst aspire to be like the other faction. I say this is the worst scenario due to damaging changes in lifestyle that might be developed - and even if not taken up, this aspiration can only lead to disappointment. You can never look like someone else, even when they're not edited. We need to be comfortable in ourselves, it's the only person we have a chance to be. Focus on that, and not someone else.

And corporations - stop selling self-hatred to get your moisturiser sales up.
The human mind and its peace can never be valued against marketing tactic and bank accounts. Teach love, don't sell shame.

Heretical Boy

Oh, heretical boy,
Of home-made secrecy made public through screens.
Adept thumbs, experts of artistically portrayed scenes.
Your heart, your love,
Never good enough to enjoy in your own time,
But pride enough in moments to share online.
The highlights. The joys.
Or the times that can be edited, played with like toys
To look so good and oh so fine, the worst of memories are all
cut in the refinement
Of what you meant by that last post.
Of the smiles and jokes that are all you seem to boast,
Forget admittance and honesty for this game of competitive
travesty,
Share stories to evoke envy, post photos to show your enemies.
Prove your relationships are alive by incessantly providing
evidence online,
But what will happen to those loves when the internet comes to
die?
When no one 'likes' the fact you are together?
Do you think those memories will continue to last forever?
They will online.
But unless you stop, and experience real life,
Everything those lights convey behind screens will shrivel, die.
Your entire internet history is already a lie.

Apathetic

Complete apathy, undo serenity
Examine quantity, define the quality
Speak intently, think directly
Abuse secretly, masturbate publicly.

Thoughts within the skull bring burns to the skin
Beliefs of the heart poisoned by the tumours sin
Agreeing to burn against the bloodlust will
Fill the zippo to crack a cheap thrill

With ginger density and peaking troughs
Crane light pollutes such obelisk stars
Inferiority expands under the sky's expanse
Iris' erode under degradations trance
Add, subtract - burn those pupils that thrive life's dance.

Self-Sufficient

In the depths of psychosis one of the hardest parts of living is experiencing your own person. Accepting who you are, why you are how are you - and why you love and loathe certain things. This is transferrable across a plethora of diagnoses. Self-hatred is no common cliché when it comes to mental disorder, many problems may be appealingly routed to the fact that we hate ourselves. This must be a false. Logically, the brain surely could not create itself merely to destroy or degrade its own existence. Children do not despise their actions, nor do they gaze into a mirror with contempt and disgust. These are learned behaviors. Mental illness in ways is evidence of the wars we have won, the scars we bare. Habitual creatures learn their habits from somewhere - we are not randomly created in a genetic lottery of who will have anorexia or BPD - these are not curses from birth. Of course, many disorders have genetic stems and travel through family DNA, Schizoaffective Disorder included. Symptoms may evolve with age - they are guaranteed to in fact, but it cruel to place blame on our own souls for such mishaps. Genetic symptoms are no fault of the self - but coping with them is the duty of the self.

Other behaviors involving self-loathing are almost always picked up. A child does not think of its weight until it is pointed out, a man is not born with the knowledge he will one day self-harm, and an older woman does not recall any inherent knowledge that she would day feel ugly. These lessons of self-depreciation are trained by society, a society designed to breed dissatisfaction. The most beautiful people in the world are hired alongside the best photographer's and editors in order to create desirable marketing schemes - setting a standard telling us to do better, work harder, eat better, push harder - be better. Modern Western society, without turning too political, is a major catalyst for the downward spiral in mental health - particularly in younger generations. Vja television, social media and magazines, young minds are carved into self-loathing by being exposed to unattainable standards of everything. Everything. Think of the News. We either only hear of stressful and horrific events worldwide or in government, or people are admonished for the way we look, the way we act. Magazine's make names for themselves by shaming celebrity's bodies and praising worthy individuals. Nobody is unworthy. We are all different.

Perhaps the hardest thing we can do is switch off from the callous acts of modern-day media as in thrives on our decline. Mental health will never improve if we constantly compare ourselves to individuals in different (usually photo shopped) circumstances. All you can do is switch off and focus on yourself. Look in the mirror. Remember when you were a child and loved the way you looked, were fascinated by every strand of hair and the way light glimmered in your iris' reflection. Be a child again. It's okay to forget some of the lessons that were hammered into as you matured. Some lessons are only meant to serve us for a short amount of time. Self-hatred may even have a use, to be the causality of some sort of humility and gratitude. But these lessons can be learned quickly and must not be dwelled upon. Shame can only ever come from other people.

When mental health antagonises the self, we must not tyrannies our mind. Follow the disgust to its route - where do these aggravated words of poison come from. It will not be from yourself. You never wanted to hate yourself. Mental health will very well impact your reality in every way, and affect every emotion you ever feel. But it has no right to make you despise your own person. Trace back. Find the fault. Blame. Release. Your feelings towards yourself are someone else's fault. That means it's okay to love yourself.

iV

The People

Life is too short to hate another human being.
You've made mistakes as well.

Paths

Today, we said goodbye.
If it had been 3 months ago, I would have worried
You were leaving me behind
But reality, and life itself, dictates
The different paths for the individuals
Gazing across at your path taught me
Invaluable lessons, and memories that will be cherished
I thank you, sincerely and hopefully
And hope that the messy cobbles of my way
Did not leave potholes in the footsteps of yours.
I can't help but dream,
I wish our paths had been a little closer
Or that the roads stretched a little further
But I am eternally grateful
That I could glimpse into your life, and
For the walk that we got to share together.

Ointment

Knowing how to help is impossible. You cannot negate trauma and cannot take it away. But there may me some things you can do to soothe a sufferer, whether practically or emotionally. When I am at my worst, I have rejected help, but I also accepted it. Times when I accepted it were when I did not have an option to refuse, if someone cooked a meal for me, if they ran me a bath, wrapped their arms around me. Small things I would never ask for. However, the common mistake here is that while I could not ask, I also could not accept an offer. If any of the above were offered to me in a question I would deny the offering. It had to be there already so I did not feel inconvenient and I couldn't have a say in whether it happened or not. That was a huge comfort: that someone was doing something nice, that they knew I would like, without me feeling like I was pestering them. However, equally important to other's kindness is not being afraid to reach out. Amanda Palmer writes in her book 'The Art of Asking' about this eponymous subject - how important it is to learn to reach out to others in various areas. The need of help regularly goes unnoticed without request - this makes sense - how could anyone know without telekinetic capabilities. Words create words. Requests create actions.

However, they may still reject the offer, so keep an eye and ear out. If the words reject but eyes accept, maybe gently push a little more. But if panic is clear, assure them it's no trouble, and you can maybe try something later.

This is a list of things that could maybe be done to assist someone recovering from trauma, just the guidelines, to make it really help and show care add a personal touch.

Practical Help:
Cook a meal.
Take them for a walk, somewhere new or a favourite spot.

Get a distraction they might like, maybe a hobby they haven't
done for a while, such as a book they never got around to
reading, new pencils or a notepad if they enjoy drawing,
Run them a bath.
Arrange doctors' appointments if applicable.
Make warm drinks.
Do a shopping run.
Be open.

Emotional Help:
Give a long hug. Ask if they prefer to be held softly or tight.
Plan a film night and get their favourite snacks.
Hold their hand.
Lead conversations.
Alternatively, just sit quietly with them. Company helps even
without words.
Be present with them.
Play with their hair or scratch their head (EVERYONE I know
loves this)
If your relationship is appropriate, let them be the little spoon.
Be open.

Comforting the Others

The people that care for us are commonly the people that know
and love us the most, the ones you will spend the most energy
and time dedicating their lives in attempt to improve yours.
They are also the ones that tend to get the least
acknowledgement for the burdens they undertake.
I have been, sadly, terrible at this.
Recognising someone's acts for you must be done - we rarely
expect strangers to help us, so why take it for granted when our
closest relations give aid?
We are owed nothing from those that love us. The love in
relationships is all that matters, and it's important to remember
that does not enforce a duty upon anyone. When someone goes
the extra mile to help you, in any way, it should always be
counted as a blessing, the kindest of gestures. Our carers could
easily focus on their own lives and pay no heed to our darkest
parts, yet make sacrifices to bring us light. We must try our
hardest not to burn them when we are on fire, and if we do, we
must attempt to reconcile and heal that wound.
Do not blame yourself for their pain, they have taken up this
cause for a reason, the reason being love. To not afflict yourself
further, merely show that love back. Show grace and gratitude.
Hold no grudge if the level of aid changes, if the tasks our carers
undertake become less frequent. Thank them for the time they
spent on you, allow them to have their own lives. They still care,
they most likely still worry. But we all follow our own paths,
and if the two have drifted slightly, this is no reason to be bitter.
This was a lesson I learned the hard way, when I never gave
heed to why my closest friend grew further from me, and I
became poisonous in order to demand more help. I was never
owed that help, especially when I was not attempting to recover
myself. They gave me patience and I gave them venom despite
all they had done for me. I, now, can never apologise enough for
my behaviour. I never meant for kindness to fuel my cruelty.

When people come and go from your life, thank them for the while you got to share together. You may crave more, but this is not your decision to make. Life will lead you in many a strange way. Hold fast, plod along, and focus on your own road. And let others do the same.

Schizoaffective disorder is so difficult to be around. The actions catalysed by illness can bring pain all around, something I wish I had known long ago. I wish I'd offered to make tea for the ones who sat with me through episodes, showed them my gratitude. Of course, reward is rarely the reason someone might choose to help you, but it's nice for the effort to be noticed. When a person is not obliged to take action, the action should be noted and remember.
I'm sorry I was never good at that.

Check on your carer, or on those that help you. They may hide things as not to worry you. Even if you cannot help them, you can be aware that they have things going on in their own lives. Do not enforce your problems that they cannot solve their own. Show your care for them as they show it to you, and if you are not capable of taking action to the same extent, show what you can. A little goes a long way. Appreciation speaks volumes. Kindness breeds kindness.

The Shove

Heave yourself unto hate
Chastise yourself for recent decisions
Kick at everything you despise
Loathe until your lungs no longer strain
And then thank yourself for taking the first steps
Towards Recovery.

Notes on Treatment

There is no one who can aid recovery. There are people and systems that aid you in helping yourself recover.
No pill, no therapy, no other person can heal you unless you desire to heal yourself.
Other's cannot build if there are no foundations.
It is excruciatingly difficult to, firstly, accept the need for help and perhaps even more difficult to go about getting the right kind.
The modern world is sadly run on 'prescribe now, treat later' sort of mentality when it comes to mental health. Waiting lists run so long they can be shortened by death, denial and fury.
People are not getting help fast enough. Thus, it becomes down to the individual to manage the wait.
This is underestimated.
People usually go to get help when they feel they are deteriorating. People often only get help when it is too late, and psychological scarring has already begun.

There is no easy way of coping in the purgatory of a waiting list. I'm currently back on one, anxious as to when I will hear back. I am hoping to restart Psychotherapy but starting to worry my current mindset is engraving its way into permanence with a chisel.

Distractions are necessary, but need to be wholly positive during this period.
If work is making you depressed, you need assess it's worth.
I've had to leave several jobs due to mental health, and it was worth it. It took away places I associated with negativity and stress.

If there is a meeting, or a lecture, or a class you really feel you can't go to, skip it. You cannot function without a mind, and if the mind is telling you absolutely cannot go, listen to it. However, you must also challenge it. On a good day, or a slightly less shitty day, do something that might challenge you. If it goes wrong, forgive yourself and move on, you learned not to do it again. If you can do it, it's a step forward. Both are good outcomes.

Look after your body, if you can. Spend some time outside, even if only a 10-minute walk. Have a nice stretch in the morning and before bed. Cook for yourself. If you can't be bothered to cook for yourself, my tactic is to invite someone round for a meal and cook for them. It feels nice to do something for someone else, and you're being kind to yourself in the process.

If you are offered medication, give it a try. Don't refute a pill because it's a pill. It might work, it might not. Medication can be trial an error. Try a few before you finally refuse it. They don't work for everyone, myself included, but I know people whom it is a saving grace for, even if it is only administered short term. Do research, and I don't mean the list of side-effects you can find online. Stories of how it impacts real people, in detail. Olanzapine (A sedative and anti-psychotic) made me exhausted and gain weight within a week of starting it, but for other's it works wonders in managing voices and mood. Other anti-psychotic medications have been hugely beneficial to me by stabilising my mood and boosting my energy, somewhat removing negative symptoms and giving me a bit of clarity and ability to function through the days a little better.

My newest venture in the 'dealing with purgatory' phase is support groups. I recently joined a support group for Eating Disorders. It's nice to meet other people who feel the same way or have similar problems. It can be heart breaking, especially in this scenario, to see such blossomed personalities loathe and punish themselves for the way they look, but it helps. Trading compliments is stupidly therapeutic, and explaining the root of problems and their manifestations brings introspection and security. It's a place to ground my mind, learn about the problem, and attempt to plateau the increasing issues before I start therapy.

All of these things can be done by you. The motivation might not exist right now. But there will be a spark, perhaps not obvious perhaps at the most unexpected of times. But it will come, and with it you can do one thing. And coping methods will snowball. And when the coping becomes less effort, therapy, or any other help you undertake, will become exciting. But it must start with your desire.

Tracing Fingertips

My first experience with EMDR was a mixture of internal brutality and prolific relinquishment. The therapy was done with my psychologist, in two-hour sessions over a handful of weeks. Before I had the opportunity to try this, I'd had a series of breakdowns and finally admitted to my father that I had been sexually abused just over a year before, and I spent that anniversary period keeping all of my emotions cooped up to myself before, naturally, they came flooding out. So due to the sadly excruciatingly long waiting lists on the NHS (a fault of our government, the NHS is mostly a place of Saints) I was lucky enough that my parents would help me get private treatment.

So, there I was. With a private psychologist, one-week post consultation. Nervous was one word. Fucking terrified was another. This was my first real experience of therapy or treatment since I had ditched my earlier sessions as soon as I was able, and was never entirely compliant with any medications. The chair was comfortable. But not in a sort of, 'you want to sit in me', more a sort of 'and now you are trapped, sink', sort of way. It was a sort of turquoise in a room pale blue. I was trying to focus on anything other than what was going said to me. The crux of the matter was; I had been repressing everything for over a year and now was going to have to focus on all of that shit, in front of a stranger.

EMDR works in way (this is going to be the most skeletal explanation of the process) where you fixate on traumatising memories, specific moments that evoke a physical reaction you. For example, I had an image of being choked, which afterwards brought tension to my neck whenever it was touched due to the trigger - thus the therapy is used to work through these triggers. I had three main areas associated with images; my neck (being choked), my stomach (being called fat) and my chest (from remembering my heart pounding at what would feel like it would break my ribcage from the inside out). As you begin to trace the finger tips and think about these images, the memories, emotions and even physical sensations are drawn back, and any repressed emotion comes back. After a while of working through (what feels like an eternity) the grips of any physical symptoms begin to falter, and the image in your mind becomes blurred. I can still remember the brief moment in which his grin faded from my mind.

The therapy is incredibly intense and horrendously difficult at moments, as there is no hiding from the trauma that has occurred, and it has to be faced head on. Most psychologists will not recommend this therapy unless you are showing stability in your mental health. However, after 3 weeks most of physical reactions to triggers were almost gone, and the moments of release felt in that moment were beautifully revealing. One second I was crying from the images in my mind, the next from joy that they were fading.

In terms of trauma recovery though, this was only half the job completed. I'd reduced physical symptoms and had a decline in flashbacks which were both hugely welcome changes. Now there was the mental game of building up self-esteem again, self-worth, relationships, coping with intimacy, learning to give and accept love. These are all things that develop with time - some of which I'm sure will be lifelong works in progress. But I will, in time, try to offer some sort of advice on building up on each of these things.

Experiences with Treatment

While I'm not trying to dissuade anyone or paint a bad picture of psychological therapy, I am going to give an honest opinion on my history with treatment - please be aware this is my own view, biased (as I have already mentioned) by my mistrust of doctors, and in no way should impact your own. With that said, I have had some very good experiences in sessions, particularly in EMDR, which I'd like to discuss more in depth later.

Therapy is a difficult topic to tackle, with so many various kinds and with so many purposes, it's hard to pinpoint the exact definition of that word. It's not all Oedipus complex's and psychoanalysis regarding your favourite colour, as some taboo's may suggest. Some of my experiences have proved incredibly helpful, friendly and fruitful. I was lucky enough to undertake CBT (Cognitive Behaviour Therapy) privately after I finished EMDR, a sort of talk therapy for tracing problems back to the root, and developing recovery from here.

I think the reason I took so long to buy into therapy was that I never did the work outside of the room, which is 80% of the battle. An hour a week cannot fix you, it merely gives you the tools that can help you rebuild yourself - if you put in the work. CBT massively helped me rebuild my levels of concentration and safety within myself. It traced my problems beyond hating myself and pinpointed where those feelings came from, which naturally came with revelations, and dissuaded me slightly for despising my every atom.

I, until recently when travelling made it impossible, attended a support group for Eating Disorders which had a special group for individuals who had suffered from trauma, and this tended to be the origin of people's conditions. It was hugely beneficial to be around individuals who has been through horrific things, but were making active effort to help themselves and undertake recovery. Even on bad days, it was an uplifting environment to be in, seeing people's progress and helping anyone who was in the midst of a struggle. I've never been diagnosed with any long-term ED, but my university recommended it to me when I was going through a particularly bad time and had resorted to starving myself in the name of self-help. This group made that time so much easier - everyone inspired each other's recovery and healed together, and when we could not, we supported and helped each other through dark hours.

Group therapy and support groups seem incredibly daunting to go to, especially if you've never been before, but I believe the benefit of being surrounded by people rebuilding themselves is one of the most humbling and inspiring experiences to be had. The smiles that could still be shared after the most grotesque stories, the tears that came with the most joyous revelations.

Other times have not been quite so conducive. As I have previously mentioned, my times being sectioned have been the worst experiences of my life, and my fire experience with therapy as a teenager put me off to the extent, I lied to get out of it. I've learned that if you're unable to trust your doctor, or treatment doesn't seem to be responsive and you can pinpoint why, that it is imperative to be open about this - adjustments can be made. Over the course of 3 years I saw a psychiatrist every couple of months and never opened up honestly about my problems, and didn't think the doctor listened or quite took me seriously. This may have been a concept of my own paranoia, but nonetheless it seriously hindered my progress in recovery. One of the main causes of my apathy was a question regarding my tattoo's being a form of self-harm. I was self-harming at the time, and this negated my ability to open about this as I began to feel like a bit of a joke in those sessions. The same questions on repeat that never did more than scratch the surface of any issues, leading me to believe I was not being heard.

I absolutely encourage anyone seeking therapy to undertake it with an open mind, be bold and brave - I definitely would be a the slight-more-stable place I am now if I hadn't undergone these treatments. But do not go in expecting any sessions to be magical cures. Just as there is no wonder-drug in medication, there is no wonder-class that will 'cure' you of any ailment in an hour. Be patient and speak your mind, be open to change, make your needs heard, and above all, work on yourself outside of meetings. Learning self-love is a full-time educational undertaking, and will not be developed in weekly sessions to the same extent as when you revise and extend that work yourself. Take your time. You deserve it. Growth is inevitable and blessed. As are you.

Show yourself the same support a professional does. Remember that whatever the circumstance, they are trying to help you. And that's exactly what you should be doing.

It's all you can.

Advice for Therapy

Build trust and believe their words. If you are unable, tell them, arrangements can be made.
Have an idea of what you might want to try.
Relating to the above - do some research.
Be open minded.
Have someone close to your heart pick you up or meet you after the first few sessions.
Don't go on an empty stomach.
Remember you can say anything.
Be completely honest, do not hide anything. A therapist or psychologist can only help to treat what they know about.
If you are given a task, do it. You might not feel any benefit, but it will help their understanding of you.
Take it at your pace, never feel pressured.
Do something for yourself before and after.
Don't be ashamed - you can tell people where you're off to.
Ask questions. You should never feel uncertain about the process.
Similarly - don't feel you have to share things with people outside of therapy.
Practice and develop your own techniques - even bullet-point or brainstorm some development idea' s or tasks post-session.

Hold hope that it is helping. It will move mountains before you are ever aware.

System of

Blood and Ink join in fusion
Syllables form to proclaim acknowledgement
Of a dirty secret all too well known
'It's not a big issue'
the mouth quivers and refuses to spit out such
Blatant anti-truths
A stern examination overcomes a steely gaze
And encouragement to open meanders its way across
The mouth curls up, more Cheshire Cat than convincing
Conducing to the density of panic,
That he who saw the body in trust
would critique the direction
In which I lean.

<u>*Cam*</u>

It happened. It's fine. It's not happening now. Squeeze.

Straw Concepts

Respect the other creatures that exist in unison with us.
Another animal's love can fill you like no other humans.
Notice the air you breathe and the release of your lungs
See the art in nature, and the callousness of certainty.
Immerse yourself in what will always be there,
Which in reality, is only two causalities:
You.
And your dreams.

That's easy to focus on.

Blame

There is no arbiter in mental health who dictates the right from the wrong. Guilt, selflessness, narcissism, responsibility and bitterness intertwine like Yin and Yang in mirages that cloud the judgement of all - not just a sufferer of diagnosed symptoms. Family and friends develop distress and sometimes trauma from another's actions - this cannot be avoided. Confusion and anger will continually be the result of unexplainable actions and bad luck. Illness could be compared to some sort of sadistic lottery. There may be statistics that 1 in 4 people suffer from diagnosed mental health conditions at some stage in life, but I would wager 4 out of 4 people have been affected by mental health - in their own heads or within their social circles. Everyone has described someone in their life as a 'psycho', and most people will know someone suffering severely - whether they know it or not.

The illusion of blame is born from lack of understanding another's problems - on both sides. There is sympathy for another party but the lack of knowledge leads to frustration. Example: Person A may never understand why Person B has attempted to commit suicide, yet acknowledges the tragic moment and attempts to console Person B. Person B's problems persist and shuts off from Person A - causing Person A to worry more, causing stress, leading to anger that they can't understand or aid Person B. This leads to either Person A blaming themselves for not being there in the past, or becoming bitterly sympathetic to Person B, acknowledging a problem but with distaste and feelings of helplessness now on both sides.

Flip this. Person B understands it is difficult for Person A to accept the events that have transpired, and acknowledges their willingness to help. However, the problem persists, and Person B can recognise Person A's frustrations, so perhaps shuts down more, or maybe opens up more - which could potentially scare Person A further. As Person A is impacted more and more, Person B catalysis the thought that they are toxic and severely impacting Person A's life and happiness - spiraling another depressive thought chain. Alternatively, person B may grow furious that Person A cannot respect the problems or desires of Person B, due to the alienation both parties feel from the other's problems.

There isn't much that can be done to avoid situations similar to this. The emotions are married to the situation, the connotations inseparable from the problem. Only small tasks can help. Listen to each other. Person B needs help Person A cannot provide, and cannot be expected to by either party. Learn each other's problems in depth. Swallow anger. Remove yourself from the situation when tension arises. Let each other breathe. Do not expect a saviour. Attempt to be open and learn. Accept it's the situation's problem, not any individuals. It's common. Grow with it.

Softening the Blow

During the most unstable periods of life it is all too easy to forget the impact our minds have on those around us. This is not something to feel guilty of, it' s bad luck lottery that many, many people have won. However, that is not to say we should ignore the moments of apathy towards those we hold dear. Most importantly in our minds we must remember they exist, have feelings and lives just as all do. These exercises cannot be forced though and sometimes, try as we might, we are unable to escape the dimensions of our own skulls. The point is merely to show you are aware of others worries. Acknowledge their emotions and not cower from what you fear they may feel. Have conversations that are directed both ways: talk with each other about each other, and never shy from honesty. I have lost connections through being unwilling to open the door as to how I might have impacted them and unable to admit I may have forced their feelings in a certain way - but this conversation must be had to preserve relationships, and to grow from bad places. Resentment often grows from denial.

One person cannot be your saviour. In reality, no one can be your saviour. Never place all of your thoughts and problems onto a single friend or family member - they are not professionals and will likely be affected by your troubles much more than you think. Rely on a few people to a lesser extent, open a safety blanket around you of people who care, but do put the pressure on them that may force excessive and unhealthy worrying. It's also much healthier for you to have multiple who know your issues, or sections of issues, rather than one person who may feel an obligation to your mind more than their own. Mental illness will attempt to make you selfish, fight that. Be selfish to an extent of self-care, but never force someone else to be selfless to the extent of burnout. Never make someone hold everything themselves. This is my greatest regret to date.

Be open. Be wholly honest about your feelings - but be wary of vocabulary. Don't be flippant about things which may crush someone who has not experienced them - or worse, has. Everyone has a mind just as complex as yours, with their own individual triggers, problems and coping mechanisms. Try to be aware of these when you speak - and in return listen. You can learn a lot and hugely further the relationship you have with someone just be being open with them, and being open to them. Even in your most distressed moments, you can comfort someone else: and I promise this will comfort you. Helping another is the greatest way to help you help yourself. It takes your focus outside of an area you hate and to something positive - something which you may love. Both parties will appreciate the smallest gesture.

When in hospital, I was atrocious at remembering that people I loved had travelled - usually during inconvenient times - to come and spend time with me. Distract, be there for, sit quietly with. No matter what the time was spent doing it was a welcome release, and one that requires serious care and effort on the other's behalf. I had looked forward to people coming to visit so much that I forgot they were taking time out of their lives for me. Be mindful of this, show appreciation during and after dark times.

<u>Save Yourself</u>

In esoteric genius, one has claimed four
But when four became two
There is only so much left to lose
And when hundreds converge on one
And one implicates two is the shield
Some holy light to divide one from zero
Two must stand to choose and stand to reason
Justify logic against empathy
If two is to divide itself once more
Then two one's will co-exist
Unable to save themselves

Present Company

Healing must be treated as a constant process, whether
conscious or not. An awareness must be kept at all times that we
are attempting to care for ourselves, and build our individual
mental strength. This includes what we do when alone, and in
company. Our companions in life are one of the largest spheres
of influence we have in life - maybe the most prominently
impacting thing we experience outside of our own minds. This
naturally includes friends, family, colleagues and maybe even
the staff at your local, depending on how often you frequent the
pub (I'd recommend if mental stability is in an erratic state,
limiting this particular trip is a good idea). The energies, moods
and particular companies of the individuals you surround
yourself with will play more of a role in your mindset than you
will realise. Toxicity can be hard to notice when you seemingly
have a solidly established and 'good' relationship with someone.
However, negative traits are frequently contagious. You may get
dragged into too many nights drinking, working jobs or shifts
you don't want to do, or even feeling obligated to see people
that you may not feel inclined to spend time with.
Bravery is a necessity in these moments - toxic relationships
must be cut out, painful jobs left and sometimes, if required,
family member's unspoken of. Of course, some future security
should be lain down before these calls are made if at all
possible, and the short-term effects may be painful and even
regretful, but as time passes you will realise you've made solid
groundwork and are moving forward. Progression is a self-
building process - it multiplies as it continues, develops as you
pursue the light - immerse yourself in those that shine alike.

Surround yourself with positivity at every possible moment. Perusing happiness may seem like a tedious and enduring effort, but it eventually becomes noticeably rewarding - recently I've started spending more time with people than in solitude - and surprisingly enjoying it. How can we heal if those around us reopen our wounds? Or block our progress? Environment is everything. The ones who are worth keeping in life are the ones who respect your needs, even if it means distance; anyone who can't accept the value of your needs in relation to their time cannot be considered valuable. Your surroundings must respect and be conducive to the healing process. There's no way to start development if there's friction stopping you from the get go.

Amphibian

Such green never to have been grazed upon,
This breeze that cools even the hottest of tempers,
A view, like beauty unforetold, staggering and breath-taking.
A breath, so fresh and full I wonder how my lungs have
stomached anything before,
A glimpse at peace, a piece of grace and heavenly faith.
Brown striped being, squatting upon all fours,
In effortless fashion sweeps it's body across the air, unto some
new floor.
I watch you croak and bend and croak again,
I see you survey your kingdom; you are the envy of men.
Brown striped beauty, you know not of your luck,
You have escaped permanently to a body; all men would kill
to...
But you know that that is the rule, the gatekeeping law of your
lands,
That all must relinquish lust, to ever be offered this hand.
This hand of God, rolling mounds acting as the muscles,
River's as creases, reeds portraying wrinkles,
And you, Little Brown, Striped Benevolence,
Are the life running through these veins.

Killer

Can you see it?
Can you feel my trust?
Trying to reach out to you?
Do you know how much I am pushing to you?
Or do you just thing I'm arrogant, ignorant,
Unappreciative delinquent.
How am I, from you?
What does your perspective tell you?
That I'm a prick, just difficult, causing problems.
Or can you really see the war inside my skull,
As I battle forces that try to stop my faith in you.

Ink

'*I don't know whether to speak to you or read you.*'
Why aren't you doing both?
These symbols hold stories,
They offer more of my conscious than my tongue ever could.
I may not wear my endeavored heart upon my sleeve,
But I invite your eyes instead to witness the wisps of my soul,
Through the art and penmanship of violent needles and hours sweated.
Do not reach out to graze these beauteous scars,
I do not wear my being to be embraced to rashly,
But to remind you that there is more beneath the layers of cells that you see,
That we hold so much more than our bodies.
That there are thousands more stories beneath this tattered skin
If only you thought to ask.
The totality of days in anguish and timid contemplation were not
Completed in the efforts, for your hand to gaze with bravo,
Nor to be summarised in quick quip and lazy grin -
'*Did those hurt?*'

The Purity of Animals

Our earthly relatives call upon all sorts of harmony when we meet with them. Often, they offer more understanding than our human counterparts, and generally listen without judgement. Animals can tell when something is amiss, they do not depend on the barriers of language to sense our deepest thoughts and turmoil's. They merely detect, and offer comfort. There is sometimes nothing more blissful than crying into angry palms, only to open them and see a dog's eyes gazing lovingly and intently into your face, offering to share its hopefulness with you. When our pets are shown loyalty, they will return it tenfold, sometimes in ways we could never entreat.
Talk to your pets. Talk to your friend's pets. Talk to the cat you pass in the street on the way to the shop. They won't judge, they will return your endeavor with content and fulfilled trust.

Well, sometimes cats will just ignore you, but they don't mean it like that. Their apathy is a sign that you should not worry as much.

I will always greatly encourage spending as much time with animals as possible - they offer no pressure, only relief. They return honesty with generosity. Or, it's just nice to give a furry beauty a wee rub on the tum-tum.

Permission

You always have permission to be helped. Every single human being does. You must always permit yourself to be helped, in anything, at any time. Everyone in life deserves to be helped, and will need something from another person at some point. Whether it be financial troubles, a decline in mental stability or a loss of motivation, it's always okay to ask for, and accept the aid of another person. If a friend or family member offers to do the slightest thing for you: let them, they offered for a reason - human's, in my experience, don't offer things that they aren't willing to do. People will be willing to make sacrifices for each other, permit them to. Even if it is just to make them feel nice about themselves (which they undoubtedly will - who doesn't enjoy doing a good thing for someone the like?), a small action from somebody can make a world of difference in how you view yourself.

It's okay to ask.

Even if it's just let a friend make you a cup of tea or preparing a meal, these small tasks make it easier to open yourself to bigger requests. The little ones can remind you that you are indeed cared for, and always have been, whether you've been able to see it or not. And if you open yourself up to these little things you can build your confidence in admitting you need more help, maybe help getting to the doctors, booking an appointment for a referral, or maybe help finding an outlet. If someone offers a listening ear, they can provide it without a dancing tongue. Take the ear, allow it to listen as your tongue flows. People, when presented with the opportunity, do enjoy to listen (as unnoticed as it may go). People will open themselves along with you. It might be therapeutic for them to care for you, and at the very least everybody enjoys learning - let your friends, or a friend, learn about you and what goes on internally. Let them express themselves internally. Ask questions and request, both are fantastic opportunities.

Help them while they help you - they might not need a much support, or maybe they do and they don't show it, but you can only find out by reaching out. Admitting you have a problem to someone could form a whole new relationship on mutual grounds. You can both learn and develop as time passes, that relationship becoming more honest with time.

It's easy to believe, especially with mental health or a lack of self-worth, that you deserve the problems occurring within yourself or in your life. Psychosis, depression, anxiety, insomnia, all afflictions: they never tell the truth. They make you believe that your life is one way and you must live it that way, you're forced into the box of yourself with only stigma for company. Reach out, break the self-professed stigma that they have caused. You would never tell someone else who was suffering that they were supposed to be that way. Never make yourself believe anything you would not say to someone you love.

If you've been through battles, allow yourself permission to be wounded. Allow yourself permission to be treated. Allow yourself permission to reach out and heal.

Basket

You were a virtue.
Personification of all that is true,
Taught me Tempest and Moose,
Reasoned my eyes of what to hold good.
You should never should have felt obligated.
You should have put yourself first long ago.
It is beautiful to watch you bloom,
From here.
Thank you for showing me who I might be.
I'm almost there.

Thorn & Stem

Rose senses something astray, Unable to place this faint tickling to any singularity of her senses but nerves unravel as her anticipation steels itself in suspense. The bags under her eyes have been weighing up for weeks - rest though she may, Rose has never found sleep.

There is no caller that keeps her wake, no suitor that stems her heart to palpitate - merely a sense. Purely, the unease.

Her thumbs have not graced the silky-smooth glass of her phone in days - 'do not disturb' is now her life. But this is no longer any meditational cleansing but now a cage, where solitude offered peace but never gave consent for release.

The LED burns her pupils, etching the lessons of self-consciousness into the textbook of her hippocampus, an overthought of fear. An overbearing lecturer.

Fear has found its place as her aphrodisiac, as the sense of unease is mixed with the smell of her sex. 'One must pass the time somehow', she whispers morosely to herself.

Locked in and drained out, with silent screams and blind, longing eyes. Rose knows she must be her own genesis. But this ghost, of name; Paranoia, has claimed her, in his sickly and ironic comfort.

Ramona (A Series of Interviews)

She sits across the table with a rare coffee in her palm, clutching it as if it resembles the holy grail. Sipping timidly, her gaze is a mixture of disdain, regret, distrust and intrigue. Her lips have not yet parted for anything but to let caffeine seep down her throat.
I select words carefully, attempting to aptly fit the silence between us to evoke some response, or vocal acknowledgement of my existence. We sit like this at length, her steely gaze reflecting any voiced provocation I can muster. I try to engage her in our mutual sufferings - I have learned of our commonality, but not through her. She evidently has no interest in this. She knows it all too well, and I imagine her creased brow is a communication of some sort, hinting that discussions of diagnoses bore and pain her.
My confidence in the situation falters. I had assumed this would be a little easier than this appears to condemn.
I know little else about her, and our barrier stands tall.
Her eyes drop to my chest.
Now it is her eyes that falter.
A glimmer of a smile plays across her face, though it touches her eyes more than her lips.
This fraction of a second has deceived her stone expression, and I deduce what has warranted this moment.
'You like poetry?'
She nods. The feature that has caught her attention is the Sylvia Plath T-Shirt I'm wearing.
Finally, a topic to latch to.
'Do you like Sylvia Plath?'
She nods. And finally offers words to me.
'Yes. The Colossus is magical.'
This makes me smile now. I haven't spoken to anyone else who's found one of the most devastating and relentless collections of poetry I've read beautiful. Nor have I before met someone with the same condition as myself.

We discuss our favourite highlights from her work, from 'Daddy' to 'The Moon and the Yew Tree' to 'Lady Lazarus'. She recites the latter to me, and when I close my eyes, I find myself transported by a woman who clearly has these words rooted in her soul with understanding.

When my eyelids beat open as she finishes, she is smiling - seemingly ironic with the words she has just brought forward, but contenting none-the-less.

'And you?', she speaks softly, with an indignant sliver of hope in her voice.

I blush a little. I might call myself a poet, but the prospect of following one of the most beautiful readings of my favourite poet's work fills me with terror, and a little shame.

I try to laugh it off, but by this point she has seen my truth.

'Yes, a little', I answer embarrassedly.

'Would you tell me some?', she requests.

Initially I decline, my confidence having truly faltered now, I wanted to know her more than share my writing.

Evidently, I have little choice, however, and make her an offering to which she agrees.

I stutter my way through the only piece I can recall in those panicking moments, and she listens attentively, patiently, devoutly.

When I end the final stanza and cough an ending, she smiles, leans back.

She begins to talk.

Ramona (ii)

It's not quite a smile that she greets me with, but definitely an acknowledgment, and one that seems to come across with a lack of loathing, upon my entrance this time.
We share a cigarette in silence before conversation ensues.
She is more open, even if only fractionally, to my questions about her condition this time: even though she limits her answers to nods and slight flinch like movement.
She speaks of having never heard silence in 23 years. I empathise to the extent I can, and we discuss this further. She describes her voices as a sort of running commentary - a narrator that obliterates any of her own decisions or actions out of her control. She winces for a moment before falling silent. She relinquishes herself to the call momentarily, eyes squinting like a child who has seen this scalding coming for a while. When she re-enters our shared reality, she looks at me with disgust - but not for me, for her situation. She diverts our conversation elsewhere, to more comfortable ground. I oblige, understanding all too well the catalyst of her change.
She asks again about my poetry, and off guard I describe my inspirations and themes - what the aim for my writing is (somehow, I manage to stammer out an answer 3 times the required length and with very little cohesive thought). She listens with her eyelids relaxedly shut, seeming to home in on my voice acutely with some driven concentration, but intent on hearing every syllable. A feeling of shame and awkwardness falls over me as I try to summarise whatever it is I do (which is hard when I've not entirely figured that out for myself), because I want to hear from her.
So, I return the question.
'Do you write?'
She shakes her head with a grin filled with some sort of smug pestilence.

'I could not critique if my work provided nothing better. It does not, so I do not.' The profoundness makes me uncomfortable, her way of words proving to be apparently directly agile, yet she does not write. And here I am, the day before having shared my own, and now sit stroking my narcissism by describing it her. She can clearly read this in my obtusely window-like eyes.

She asks for another cigarette, with an 'it's okay' intention in her voice. She winces again. I can see her pain, so I try to let it settle. I know sympathy will do nothing. I return the it's okay in my smile, and offer my lighter in the only gesture of care I have in my arsenal.

Again, we smoke in silence. I can read this is a ritual for her - she does not want to mix words with tobacco. The drawing of smoke brings her a form of clarity, I think, that brings a rare relaxation for her.

I'm acutely aware we only have a few minutes left. Unbeknown to me, so is she.

She stubs her cigarette with mysterious intent and stares at me for several moments, considering.

She reaches her decision with a stern look and parts her lips.

'I have a request.'

Ramona (iii)

We reach an accord: I promise to fulfil her favour if she expands
my repertoire. She obliges.
She tells me tales from throughout her life, from her earliest
memories, to months that never took place.
She talks of a tragic youth; her early diagnosis made her fall
victim to bad people.
She was confirmed to hold delusion and hallucinations with
conviction from a young age, it made her a target.
No one believed her when she said she was molested. A heavy
example of how sufferers of mental illness often become victims
of mental illness rather than perpetrators.
Her first attempt at ligature came at the age of 17. She was
sectioned after surviving, and has never removed the label of
'danger to herself',

Despite this, she can laugh honestly. Her demons do not entirely
drown her being - they are more like waves that pull her
underwater often, but occasionally (and thankfully) she can
make her head break free for air.
She holds no remorse nor self-pity, she is entirely accepting of
her situation, and who she is.
She still wants to die however. Just because she doesn't hate
herself, it doesn't mean she wants to live her life. At some point
she emphasizes that just because you have a good soul it does
not mean life is uncruel.

She tells me all this with a gratuitous air of nonchalance. She
lights a cigarette to signify the ending of what she is willing to
share with me, for the moment, and closes her eyes.
I get the feeling she is willing to share more: regrettably
however, she is unable to.
Her words have been internally negated by an arbiter with more
jurisdiction over her tongue than she.

She leans back and closes her eyes. There's a brief smile but it is swallowed almost instantly.

When her eyes peel open again, it is clear indication that our meeting is over.

The Ballad of Rose

Rose was a girl with stars in her eyes,
Rose was a woman who was ordered to lie,
To her family and her friends and to herself and to her Gods,
The dictator that demanded this order, was her own mind.
An unshakeable abscess and cyst on her life,
With thoughts of self-mutilation her thoughts became rife:
So, her dexterous fingers slid down her innocent throat,
But from another mind that penned the note that she wrote,
That the weight of her mind pressed upon the weight of her body
And she could no longer wait for a comfortable date
And the doctors called emergency far too late
And found out, years after, that the catalyst was rape.

So, Rose never ate a bite and could do nothing but fight,
As she craved nothing more than the dying of the light.
So, tubes were forced down her innocent throat
And they went deeper than those fingers, and the words that
they wrote.
She gagged and she shrieked as they forced it inside,
Remembering once again when her legs were forced wide
So, she was restrained so fast that her eyes could barely cry
Interrogating furiously if she would ever feel alive.

Six months pass and Rose has withered to the bone,
Demons feed her lies that her weight will leave her alone.
Her friends and her family try to convene in aid,
Praying to a force above that her soul could be saved.
But God could not undo such a damage of the devil,
It was down to Rose alone, to find a life where she would revel.

Rose demanded the tubes be removed from her mouth,
And with all strength of will, she put food to her mouth,
And with all courage and rage, she kept it in her mouth
And though the devil cried in fury, she kept it in her mouth.

Now Rose has come so far, all that's left is to swallow,

*After endless months of starvation and her bones turning
hollow.
She finds strength, and hope and faith to stomach another
morsel,
And after it goes down, she goes to war with her soul.*

*For oncoming months, her conscious schemes and connives,
The lies about her waist still trying to ruin her life.
But Rose will not be undone. Rose see's light in the sun.
Rose has become the lotus flower, and she is blooming with
love.*

Ramona (iV)

I read her this poem I had written under her commission. As I read, nervously recounting the fusion of her story with my tongue, I am increasingly aware of the imperfections in its writings and delivery. She watches with intimidating ease. Leant back, cross legged, one arm swung round the back her chair and the other brandishing an ash-laden cigarette (as per usual), and her gently nudged back, her eyes calmly, intimately shut. It's hard to decipher whether she is intently listening, or devotedly ignoring. I sweat and stammer my way through each stress-inducing syllable with no want of a smile near my lips.
I am terrified. I am utterly envious of her calm.
I am more than half expecting her to wince at dreary phrases or flinch at discrepancies or inaccuracies, but she merely stays stoic and meditative until I utter the final stanza, my voice truly faltering now. This is a moment of reckoning. My rhyming is cheap.

She wrenches her eyes open sharply and stares at me with ambiguous subtext. She leans forward and puts her cigarette out on the table - for the first time neglecting the ashtray that sits in no-mans-land between us. She stays in her new position, the filter of a Marlboro Red pressed as a hostage against the plastic decadence.

She weeps. Tenderly. It is a cry I have never witnessed before; streams of salt filled tears slide down her face like a paraglider, her eyes sting red within seconds - but she heaves not. Her breathing is calm, composed. I am certain I detect, satisfaction? I do not move, I can tell she needs only a witness for this purge of emotion, anything else would ruin this moment. She draws a sharp breath and wipes her eyes, blinks twice, and sighs.
This is my invitation to speak.
'Is it okay?'
She smiles the most solemn and heart-wrenching smile I have ever had the honor of witnessing.
'It, is it. It is all that is needed.'

Ramona (V)

We part ways for the last time. We are aware we shall not meet
again, thus we wish each other the best on our path's.
We both cry now, and shake hands, thank each other. There is
far more understanding between one another than anyone, for
my part at least, I have met. As though we had shared a life. The
only other I have known to have glimpsed my reality.
She gives instructions on the words I will use.
She pauses for a second, she finds it imperative to give herself
the most suitable identity. Her eyes center on a stone next to her
left foot. She is decided.
'Name me Ramona.'

V

The Relapse

The decline is not when you feel yourself getting worse
But when the stabilisers, once more, become a struggle
That feels unworthy of bearing.

Sensory Displacement

See what you see
Hear what you hear
Feel what you feel
Say what you say
Live what you live
I despise how different
Our senses are.

Just Crossing

I am a traffic island. People wait with me for a bit, until they
can get to where they want to go.
But that's okay, because if they saw me and did begin to slow,
They'd realise that I would only drag them down,
So, I guess it's good for them
That the never stick
Around.
Or maybe they do,
And my sight is selective.

Harmony in Hate

*Tongue like a pickaxe, relentlessly pounding the concave lens of
my inner eye,
Blinding like anthrax, the smoke from those whispers clouding
vision with lies.
Those words are my own, and yet they are not.
Those are the truths I tell myself when the lies make my teeth
rot.
Hope can only ever be born from doubt, and it's in hope's oasis
that I find myself in drought,
From the refreshing respite of clarity and light, I find myself
ravaged and starved by a force that I cannot fight.
Against my own mind I feel have the muscles of a foetus,
I am unable to allow anyone else in to see this, for I am my own
prison guard,
And I may argue it's living recklessly but this is self-destruction,
The addiction above all else I could never kick.
I spout my words like they are prophecy but I ignore my own
religion.
I speak my words like gospel and yet I can never stick to them.
Standing in the world's parallel requiem, the anguish of
Antigone blinding my ears.
My eyes are dead lenses, a broken camera that only produces a
cracked blackness.
My mind a fluctuating record, that repeats the same words
indefinitely,
But increases the harshness of its melody every day, without
fail.*

Jester

There is a man in the window. I'm on the second floor and this figure is not quite a man, like a twice dimensional husk of a being. In the window - allow me to clarify, he is not on the other side. But this paper-boned behemoth is traced in the glass itself, his hand stroking his prison wall, begging to be unleashed.
I could break the glass. Stop writing, and throw something. But his image puts me off.
A twisted smile and crimson running from his eyes, what i can only assume to be teardrops of copper scented streams.
He's laughing. I believe he can recognise my predicament as it's plasters itself onto my facial expression.
He doesn't appear inherently bad, just, unpleasant.
Maybe it's just his aesthetics that appear to be broken, his intent good and pure.
His laugh sounds vaguely familiar. Something from years ago, but I can't place it.

Do I let him out?
When I try and ignore him, he taps to call me to attention. I would love to know how he got there. How long this phantom or mirage or man has been held in his skinny cage. He refuses to speak until I let him out - at least this is what I can guess from his giggling response to any questions I have put forward.

He wasn't there. The phantom has disappeared and I cut my feet on the glass.
It was a mirror.
I did not know my own distorted face or voice.
I'm more exhausted than frustrated.

I'd better buy a new one.

The Reason

Doctors and hospitals are there to help you, they can save lives, do wonders and build you.
However, I will explain the reasons I hate hospitals and distrust doctors: Not to break your trust with, I really believe they are places for miracles, but to show what problems need seriously developed.

I have been hospitalised to Psychiatric Wards twice in my life. I have been hospitalised for suicide attempts numerous times.

My first stint in a Psychiatric Ward came two weeks after attempting to jump off a bride, where I was taken in by the police, then to my parent's home and put on a Crisis Team (a team of mental health workers that visit daily to check progress). After two weeks with them the brought a doctor for an evaluation, was taken to a place called Carseview, in Dundee. I was only in for one week thankfully, with daily visits from friends and parents, and met some lovely souls on the ward. While this sounds positive, it was far from a hopeful experience. On my first day I spent almost all of my time in my room, eventually venturing outside for a cigarette. I was approached by a woman, maybe 35 years old, who asked me why I was there and what was wrong with me. I explained I was undiagnosed at this point but suffered from rapid mood swings and psychosis, and in return asked her problems and how long she had been there. She told me 3 months, and followed this with the worst advice I had ever been given.
'They only let you out if you seem normal.'
Looking back, obviously this is a disastrous tactic: you can't get better if you're faking, doctors can't help if you lie to them. However, at the time I was 3 months from finishing college, and was desperate not to fuck it up.
It fucked up.

The next day I emailed my lecturer/director (I was studying Acting and Performance) to explain the situation. We were 3 weeks away from the play we were performing. I didn't know when I would get out. We came to the decision together to cut me from it, meaning I would fail that module, and likely have to wait another year to resit to gain my diploma. The next few days were heart-breaking, but I couldn't show it. I wanted out so I could sort my life, hospital and the doctors were stopping me from doing that.

Over the next couple of days, I met more patients. John was a very sweet older gentleman suffering from PTSD induced psychosis, and we bonded a lot over similar symptoms. He struggled to hold concentration so we kept our conversations short but frequent, usually about books that we were reading (or attempting to) and the stories of his life. He sat on his own in the garden most days, smoking and gazing blankly at a page of words he couldn't quite focus on. But he did it every day. His determination to read more than a page a day was astounding.

I met another older gentleman. I miss him dearly. He never spoke about his problems, and amazed everyone with an air lightness and laughter, which some people found infuriating, but I enjoyed his company. He made the days go quicker. We bonded over music and our love of Groucho's, an old record shop in Dundee. He was the most sensational artist I had ever seen, drawing requests for the other patients, with the most exquisite and well executed artistry I had ever seen. I asked for a vixen and her cubs, and he began. The next day I was told I could go home, and while waiting for my parents to pick me up, we exchanged phone numbers. He thought he would be out soon, as he said he felt great, and we would meet for a coffee, a browse in the battered old infamous record shop, and I could get his drawing.

Around a month later I text him, to see if he was around. A few days after he replied, saying he would 'perchance see me for a cuppa and a vinyl very soon'. Excitement flowed. I was feeling a little better, despite faking it to the doctors and crisis teams and friends and family. Medication was starting to help a little and was starting to sort things out with college, where I would be given extensions on some modules and would work on another play with a few others over the first few weeks of summer. It was working out.

I can't remember how long after that, but relatively soon after, I saw in a local paper (well, the online version of a local paper), that the artist, my friend, had committed suicide.

I learned that day that I was lucky the advice hadn't completely failed me, that I had eventually felt better after I left Carseview, but no one wants to be in that place. So, people fake. People lie. People pretend. People die. If life is some sort of purgatory that we want to escape, psychiatric wards can be, not always, but can be a hell that push people to that escape, no matter how 'fine' they seem.

This was the better of my experiences. The following account was recent, traumatic, and has ruined my relationship with professional help for the foreseeable future. Please be warned, it is graphic. I would urge anyone who already has trust issues with medical professionals to not read this, I don't think it will be beneficial for you, this is merely a form of catharsis for me to explain why I can no longer trust doctors etc.

In September 2018, I moved to Manchester for University. In the next weeks, I made no friends, was still suffering from major mental health problems but now had left all support behind, and had no motivation for this 'new start'. I felt trapped, I had no life in Dundee and in my attempt to escape, I moved somewhere which seemed unwilling to give a try. I struggled and stressed about my course instantly, I found people competitive and difficult to get along with and had no one to talk about my feelings to. I skipped classes. I fell back into bad habits. I was taken to A&E and put on a crisis team the next week. On Friday the 2nd of November, my routine broke. I made the decision. I had been having around 2 break downs every day, each worse than the last. I planned it out. I went out, bought heavy duty duct tape and 3 packets of paracetamol, something I'd tried before but this time I knew how to work it. When I got home, I began. I drank, snorted, combined paracetamol with Zopiclone (sleeping pills I had begged the crisis team for a week prior). I wanted to ensure the job. I strapped the duct tape to the pipe on my roof holding the fire alarm, for extra support. I put 2 belts around the pipe, in case I broke one. I put my head through the belt and kicked the chair. The pipe wrenched itself out of the ceiling. I felt calm. That had failed, but the pills would work. I eventually went to bed, with new found peace, and slept, certain I wouldn't wake up.

I did.
The following Monday (Bonfire Night) the Crisis Team took me to A&E to be held while paperwork was done for me to put into a Psychiatric Ward.
They did a blood test, and found severe liver damage. I freaked out, screamed and tried to leave. They force fed me diazepam to calm me.
I spent 24 hours strapped to toxic drip to destroy the paracetamol that was still in my blood, which was in the process of killing the fucking liver that was trying to keep me alive.
It was agony. It was exhausting.

So, Wednesday comes. I'm off the drip, a mental health nurse comes. I hadn't eaten because the hospital had severely limited food for dietary requirements, and I had no one to visit me. I am told that I will be moved to a Psychiatric Ward, and she would be back within 2 hours to update me.

By Friday night, she still hasn't returned, despite me asking the ward nurses to call every day.

By this point I have eaten one meal: plain rice. I have not slept due to stress.

Saturday morning, at 2am, the patient in the bed next to me with Dementia, starts screaming, He is ignored.

6:30 am, he is still screaming. I pack my rucksack and try to leave. I am forced to stay under the promise the mental health team will be round to talk to me at 8am. I hold the little hope I have left.

8 am comes.

Then 9 am.

Then 10:30 am.

At 11 am, I ask where they are. A nurse tells me that the mental health team don't work on weekends, so they should be round Monday.

I cannot describe my emotions beyond the word fury, but this encompasses nothing compared to the depth of the tsunami that washed over me.

Advice for anyone who is helping someone with mental health: Don't bullshit them.

Saturday night I had a visit from two friends which was lovely, one a surprise trip all the way from Dundee. They brought me my first proper meal in a week. Fast forward to Tuesday and I felt like a shell of the person I was. I trusted no one, I was convinced I was dead - or that the doctors were detaining me so they could kill me. That evening I was transferred to a Psychiatric Ward at long last.

This is when things slid downhill even more. Out of the frying pan and into the shit.

I arrived around 11pm and was put into a room with 3 other men. On my first night one of them tried to get into bed with me.

A doctor told me I was there to start medication and be monitored only for a few days to make sure I didn't have a bad reaction. Over the coming days I felt terrified of some patients, and the ones I got on with left within 24 hours of my arrival. By now I had missed 2 weeks of University and was pretty fucking stressed. I was getting worse. So, I went back to the old tactic. I lied to show I was better. They had all lied to me, why shouldn't I do the same?

On Friday I had an assessment and was to be discharged. Without medication - that would be sorted by a Crisis Team when I left. Another lie, I wasn't there for medication at all.

When I was discharged, I spent the next two weeks closing myself to the Crisis Team before I refused to see them again.

After what happened, I knew I was better on my own.

But never negate the help you need.
Hospital can be a horrible experience, but it can save your life. It has saved many. This is perhaps just an account of a very unlucky experience.
If you want a contrasting hospital experience that's far more in depth, read Seconds to Snap by Tina McGuff.
It goes through all sides of the experience, not just my filtered-by-distrust account.

Exhale

Are mental breakdowns the minds way of trying to purge mental illness?
Those tears, filled with depression as they long to hit the ground
Drops, filled with sadness, longing for the floor
I watched my tear fall off my cheek and I swear,
I heard the faintest cry of joy erupt as it was absorbed by this stained carpet
How dare this carpet feel no sympathy,
As a being filled only with my regrets could only find contentment
In its own destruction
Because of how I am,
This makes me a creator of sadness
As my body attempts to shake voices away, to knock them out of my skull
And my heart tries to beat anxiety in a race
I gaze into a mirror of contortion
For it must be a wall of illusion
For that is not my face
I cannot tell if I am losing or gaining weight
My face is red and puffy but my bones seem as if they are trying to erode away my skin
To be set free
And yet I feel a need to grant their wish, to let them feel oxygen on their smooth exterior
As I cease to cry, my mind has purged, cleansed and released.
I remember
I was born to be human
Not a skeleton
But I know, fight as I might,
Soon this thought will fade.

Carnivorous Eyes

I stand, donned in a dirty towel and dusty glasses, in front of the mirror, full body, a mixture of the showers residue and my already fear-induced sweat dripping from my brow. The glass of the mirror is cracked, it seems. This has previously gone unnoticed, but evidently this was due to my ignorance, nothing more. The break seems deeper than the actual glass, it stretches back further. It doesn't, of course. It can't. Yet it does. It shines with some charmed obsidian, both tantalising and terrifying. It evokes panic and desire. Breaking my eyes away from seductive black, I notice for the first time the face that it has split in two. It's despondent. It's desperate. It's weak and pleading. I feel nothing but contempt for it. It cries at me, it's tears seem to be the most human thing I've seen in weeks, but I am aware this cannot be so. There is no crack, no doorway to this face, no false tears.
I desire to walk away, but the black won't let me. The crack commands to be witnessed, it demands an audience. I oblige, step forward. The crack seems to suck me closer, drawing my soul to be absorbed. As my fingers reach out, it closes. The face is whole. It still cries but it's tears are dry. They still fall, but they are not of fluid, not of humanity.
He looks furious and starving, like my conscious could feed his appetite.
Oh.
That's my face.
I did not recognise its colossus or malcontent. I visibly weep toxins, abhorrently.
What does that mean?

This is when I got dressed.

Incompatible

The mind & body cannot relate,
When in opposition they unify
In hate.

Staggering Iris

He's staring again. I lay in bed, dark, but enough window light
to make out Benjamin's face in the window. We've been talking
for a while, I think. Maybe 5 minutes, perhaps 15 hours. I see
we've been talking. His responses are, as per usual, limited to
vacant glares and war-filled exhalations. I've been trying to
evoke some sort of response. I've been trying to talk about love,
death, my image of myself and his image of me. He doesn't
need words to answer this final topic. I know he hates me. So
why stick around? His presence is exhausting and the voices
clamor behind my eyebrows. I cannot sleep nor dream nor see.
Like a thousand tiny snakes coiling and squirming in glorious
wretchedness, degradation spins around my head like an
enclosing noose. I'm so tired. I can barely keep my eyes open
but whenever they shut the screams stab louder. I want to eat.
To get out of bed.
I can't. The laws have been set: I am not allowed to move off of
this memory-foamed prison. I want to wash. To put clothes on. I
can't.
Everything hurts. Not physically. My thighs feel like they are
grieving, my hands in the pits of despair. I always thought only
the mind could translate emotion. My limbs have discovered an
entire new language of feeling. My condition is fluent but I am
no such thing. I can't even speak my own tongue right now.
The heat my insides is unbearable compared to my frozen skin.
Oh, let me move, I beg. I beg. I beg.

Groundwork

Today, I write from the floor, where I have not been able to tear myself away from for hours now. The motivation it took to drag myself to the laptop felt similar to the efforts of Sisyphus. I am not cursed like him, however. Sisyphus is one the greatest tragedies in ancient Greek mythology, his daily tax to push a momentous boulder to the top of a hill only to watch it roll back to the bottom, repeated for eternity. Thankfully, today's effort will not be my life. Despite weight I must look at the sun peeking through the window and know, or hope, that I will sit in its light soon. I do not want it now, but I will. Bad day's only last 24 hours, and lead to better minutes.

The floor is a good place to be. It's sturdy. Supportive. Good for me back. The carpet is soft and warm, it feels heavenly between my fingertips. This is a good place to be. I can feel the details and the pleasures in where I am. No movement necessary. Just me and a ceiling. I like the patterns in it, the straight lines that have been chamfered at the edges, the Victorian... things in the middle of squares. The way the light hangs down, centred above my forehead. If it were to fall, it would break in my eyes. Every now and then, I urge it to.

Even the cats have gotten bored of lazing around with me. I wanted to shriek as I opened my laptop back up again. I want to scream for hours that I have not closed it again yet. I don't want to do anything but lie on the floor. I hate everything else. That ceiling and this carpet are my only friends now. They can not

Skeleton Cravings

Bones erode the flesh, for
The first, he feels beautiful
And yet he still writhes
Albeit, struggling to write
A pen's weight equal to the forearm

Talking Good with Doc

I know and regret all
of my self-professed moments
of ill-informed genius and reactions of angst
And wrongfully attempted retribution.
I play them back. I rewind, and pause.
And I delve into the intricacies of my fabricated worries
Portrayed ruthlessly, terrorising the person I was.
I am aware
A self-important, misled, mistakenly indulgent
Un-prolific fool.
And now,
All that has changed
Is an expansion of vocabulary
So, I can make the same brash decisions that haunt me
When I speak
Only this time,
I can articulate my self-loathing and distrust more efficiently

Sickle

I lust for a life
Outside the confinement of death
I crave a rapture
That takes me out of purgatory
Separation anxiety is hollow
like how a spine shuddering scream is calming

I pray for existence
Outside of my mind
I hope for contentment
In somebody else's eyes
Dissociation is a reality
Sensitivity is not a weakness

First came the machines
Then away the humans went
Force fed me pills
And then left me with death
He offered out a hand
The suffocation made me calm
He wrapped me in his arms
And the bleakness made me whole
He had an opaque sort of existence
But still the only thing vivid enough to be real

Six long days past
With beeps and screams and hate
Death said I wasn't ready
That they would fix me yet
He cut me with a sickle
And claimed I hadn't earned the scythe
He wrapped me in poison ivy
And said that I my suffering was not over
Death promised, life is trying her hardest
But it's hard, when she doesn't like you very much

Enter the weight of knowledge
Enter those which kept my trust
But their intentions seemed ill
And my hope rapidly began to rust
After they promised my rectification
The came for my sanity
After the promised to build me up
They broke me further, left me a ruined man

Now I sit at home
With dust and cuts from a sickle
Silently screaming for help
With no one to confess to
They shut me out
They shut me down
They shattered my trust
And now I am alone
They tied the noose
And now they want to kick the chair

Infernal Cortex

The inside of my skull is on fire. I can see and hear reality all
around me but I cannot enjoy it. No matter how much I reach
for it, it touches me not.
This is the side of schizoaffective disorder that people often
neglect in their thoughts, largely due to a lack of information.
Psychosis is not the only problem, the agitation of mood can
occasionally be even more impacting, or frustrating, than other
symptoms. The past few days I have felt like I'm wasting hours
of my life to episodes of depression or mania. Life is good and I
can think that, but it does nothing but aggravate my emotions
more. The real killing of happiness comes from the knowledge
that it should be there. The means are practiced and the method
is there, but the invitation to feel is not. I can't tell if my brain is
burning or if it's scarred from its previous flames.
The depression has turned to anger in spite of my wishes and I
have found myself standing in a rage I cannot contain with ease;
it takes all of my energy to contain my resentment - rendering
me unable to do anything except withhold breaking. It is
exhausting, and debilitating, and demanding, and sadly, a
necessary evil.
If I speak a flood will unveil itself. If I move faster than a crawl,
I won't stop breaking everything in sight.
Oh, to actually feel the warmth of the sun I sit in.
What a dream that would be.
I feel like I've recovered from losing my mind but lost some
concepts along the way. The concept of light. The concept of
contentment. Now I can only maintain stability by releasing my
resentment.
The grey is colossal - like a war of shades in the sky waging
their battles over who can cover the sun the most.
It makes me ungrateful, spiteful, difficult.
I don't want this to be the person I am now.
Evidently there is more work to be done - it's difficult to find
the motivation or the means, however, when you feel like you're
doing all you can already. This was meant to be a break for me.
A respite. A holiday.

I don't want to despise holidays. I don't want to need distraction every instant of my life. I want to sit with my eyes closed and not see the black behind my eyelids.
I want them to still see that everything is okay.

I have become impatient. I get angry at the hope for the future and its lack of haste to come to me. There are many exciting things to come that I want now - a lack of virtue, I know. But waiting for bliss when living in disarray only makes the good toxic. Depression steals virtue. It takes the willingness to wait. It demands to be fed a release in every moment. But I cannot offer it any delicacy or milestone or event right now, I can only make it wait.
And thus, it feeds upon me instead.
Fuck you, you hungry, hungry beast.

Embers (are only pretty when they come from campfires)

There is a boy, a boy who calls himself a poet
Who almost believes it. Deny.
A boy of venal atrocities, but with a pen which transforms sins
into art
As if the sun began to absorb the Earth in its insatiable heat
Bringing an ending to all known life, all known life
But even after the death of all,
It still gave off a light of such radiance
As if beauty could negate an abyss
As if confession could reverse lies
Of such heinous proportion

Tongue's which move eloquently
Are the most masterful at deceit
And the lips become addicted to such movements
Even when the words catch themselves in the throat
But the lungs force them forward regardless

The fault of Icarus was his hubris
The fault of the boy was that he assumed
His schemes outranked his morals
On some incarnated hierarchy

Oddity Road

Help-less.
Less help than stress deserves
As friends speak of genetics embodied together
A separate being walks his boulevard with
An entity on his heart, growing and spurting,
Recoiling and throbbing
On this alley of bliss
Where relations are lit by streetlights of a future
He skulks in shaded corners, watching,
Longing,
Claimed by some history.

Three steps further down Oddity Road,
A heart with no one to kiss,
A thorn with no thistle.

<u>ng</u>

My soul is scratching my throat, mangling my vocal cords in efforts to force forward a scream with such brutality the lowest pits of hell would beg for silence. There is sometimes clarity in isolation for me, usually in fact. Right now, however, I can no longer recall the definition of alone. Faces peer through a mirror despite a black sky endlessly blinding all from sight, except ghosts that sit 30ft above the ground for the sole purpose of tormenting a tired mind. Not tired. Somewhere between needing stimulant or tranquilliser, unable to decide between sleep or activity, a mind torn in polarities of discontent and war.

My thoughts stand witness to a war of foul of demons and fouler demons wrestling for my consciousness' attention. My thoughts are commanded by neither of these sides, but only the cataclysmic recline of these sides tearing up the fabrics of my sanity.

Reality slips. I am not myself. Mirrors lie, as do voices. But the words of demons burn away any near-angelic or calming thought my cortex can muster. I lay in the trench of this battleground. I am unable to move. I am blind to anything holding resemblance of truth. I am deaf to any sound outside of my skull.

Where am I?

Who
Was
I
or
he?

Creature

Beast inside, Devil that resides
Drown my faith in bloody ravines
You're in the skin, you're in my bone
Forced from someone else's sins, to atone

Demon within, neglect his kin
Let mouths whisper no name but yours
Purest of scum, cleanest of whore's
Take him from reality in which he's bored
Burn his face, Rape his faith
Leave his blood boiled in disgrace
Then leave that place, where you take your rest
Climb to the shoulder where you can torture him best

Internal monster, are you coming closer?
Did you find the spot where you could cosy up in?
Plaguing eternity. Dissolve his femininity.
Enslave him in shame for his soul inside,
Because you don't want to share his body,
Do you - oh Creature that resides.

Cain

A man. A man of whom is constructed with more psychosis than self, a man whose image in the mirror is bereft - staggering secretly with his homemade delinquency - searching delicately for a way to be free. Free from condemning screams and intoxication sheets - every night he seems to fall to his knees and pray for release, every night he forgets the light that he tries so hard to see.

A man. A man who believe he has already passed the door of death, wanders at night struggling to find rest, a man who has become too hard to externally impress that he starts to admit that he is feeling depressed. It's a weighty blow to take, especially when in his sanity he has so much at stake - a final admittance might be the end of him, as he runs with clench fists and negates the abyss which tries to claw him from within, a devil who's grin he cannot bear any longer.

A man. Let's call him Cain. A fitting name for an anarchist of such proportion, a kleptomaniac of the literal and metaphorical, a murderer of the brothers who trusted him and the women he put faith in. Now we could call Cain an exploding calamity, a self-made travesty, a man clutching at sanity. But Cain is in need of something he deserves - he'll deny this, yes, he'll deny himself the slightest shred of contentment.

*For you see Cain is plagued by these people in his head, a
constant dread than rejects him from leaving his bed - and he
feels like everything he wants to say has already been said by
those with more fruitful tongues and far more prospering pens.
By this point Cain can no longer recall the absence of internal
chaos. Cain, in himself, a man who wants to love, a man who
wants to touch gently, kiss softly, a man who could never give
enough. But he can never give enough. He struggles to give
anything. In every love he's ever made he centred himself and
dreamed of the other, presence was lacking so he started
attacking and pulling away at the threads of a heart, a heart he
desperately wanted to hold and caress, but he was so focussed
on selfishness. And as if feasting on this weakness, Cain's
Achilles' heel, those people in Cain's head were able to twist
and steal his desires from him, turn love to hate with mere
perspective, change this new found villain's motive to love to
indulgent lust, never offering anything enough and never
changing, but merely rearranging the detestable parts of himself
so they were perhaps less recognisable. But they never strayed,
never kept away for long. And so, pestilence and pollution
became the gods which Cain adored, blinded by his hope of love
and life, he could never see he was building the factories of
misery and strife. And eventually love let go and Cain was
destroyed by this, the whole future in his eyes was torn from
bliss. But in the months that followed Cain released who he had
been, the love that he had seen and how he had wrecked it in
accord. That the fault was his own and it was time. Time that he
had to grow.
And grow he has done. Cain has grown remarkably well - he is
taller in mind and broader in thought - he is no longer selling
the lies that people bought. But every now and then, he falls
back towards pestilence and pollution, redirected however on
the self, and not to those he swore to protect. And they make him
play the most excruciating games.
Oh Cain, a man. A man who still, on the best of days, struggles,
even still, to remember his birth given name.*

The Jump

I am now going to attempt to document as much of my worst
suicide attempt to date, as much as I can remember. Or rather,
the emotions and experiences that occurred rather than a
timeline of what happened. A little over a year ago, I jumped
from a 40ft window in what I thought might be my death. What,
at the time, I hoped would be my death. I often have flashbacks
to the various moments that took place. I don't remember how I
got there. But I stood tall, shaking, on the ledge of my flat
windowsill. I was in the living room. Our kitten stared at me
from the other side of the room. Maybe he could sense what was
about to occur - knew to keep his distance. As I stood with one
hand on my aching stomach and one hand on the window handle
next to me, I saw a woman. Our neighbor from across the street,
though I could never recall seeing her before that moment. She
was on the phone, staring at me with pleading eyes and
motioning her hand for me to step back, away from danger. I
swore I heard her voice whisper in my ear. I could read her lips,
hear her thoughts. I believed she was urging me forward. Her
face brought me peace. It made me strong. I stepped with eyes
closed.

And fell.
And fell.
And fell.
And opened my eyes, thinking I was flying.
This is the moment I hit the ground. The sound of a vertebrae
being pulverised echoed in the street, or at least in my ears.
There was silence in my head. My lungs, winded as they were,
could not stop forcing air out of me at such velocity I screamed.
And couldn't stop. I wasn't screaming from the pain. Of course,
mostly I was. But for me I was shrieking at my consciousness,
my aliveness. My desperation had failed, and now all I knew
was fear of the future.

Within seconds I heard my flat mates' voice, in tears. All I could do was to scream apologies at him. I tried to run, but two steps in and I lay crumpled, dressed in the clothes I had chosen to die in.

When the ambulance came, those clothes were cut off of me. And I lay in boxers and tinfoil, with a morphine filled needle sticking out of my arm, sobbing for mercy. Praying for a heart attack. Petrified of the next minutes if I stayed alive. My heart hurt the most, despite all the other pain. From the broken spine and the cuts on my eye from where my knee collided with my face. I lay in my own blood and sweat and tears and begged for release.
No such luck.
The rest is history. Two weeks spent in bed, unable to move. Unable to shit. Unable to piss. Unable to sneeze without an agonising motion. Followed by 12 weeks in a brace, restricted mobility and crawling like a baby when it was off. I've never felt so pathetic. One morning I woke and threw up all over my room - my brace at the bottom of the bed, out of reach. One afternoon I sneezed, and screamed like a whipped dog. It's the tiny moments that last. But not just the images - every single sensation of those certain seconds is recalled. The catheter being ripped out. The look on my flat mates' face. The look of sorrow on my best friend as she walked into the hospital ward in Glasgow. The proximity of the ground to my eyes as the opened. The uncertainty of knowing if it was my decision to jump.

Everyone tells me how lucky I am. This is true. One year on and I'm fully mobile with little hindrance, beyond the aches of carrying things. I can walk, I can dance, I can smile. But if I was lucky, I wouldn't have thrown myself out that window, with a kitten sat gazing.

The Spark

The spark,
The shot in the dark,
The impulse,
The opportunity,
The moment, lingering,
Never fading, rain cascading.
It's a grey Sunday night,
Fight the dying of the light.
The idea of jumping out a window wouldn't cross normal minds
And if only people listened when Frank Turner said Be More
Kind
But who the fuck listens to folk/punk anyway?
If I played him my own mother would refuse to stay.

10 things that crossed my mind when I jumped out of a 40 ft.
building
1. Fuck.
2. This is going to hurt.
3. I'm sorry Mum and I'm sorry Dad
4. I'm sorry to the woman watching
5. I can't fly
6. Why did I put on my docs for this?
7. Am I having a heart attack?
8. I'm falling fast.
9. This is going to hurt.
10. That hurt.

The precipitancy of falling is strange
You don't go into an abyss for the deranged
You seem pure for a second, holy
And yeah, my jeans were pretty holy when they cut them off me
And the cut on my left eye meant I couldn't see
But I felt holy

Falling

Transcendent
Despondent
Emotional

And it's not like I'm an amateur to surviving attempts
But this time I really jumped with intent
And those rumors of blame are not true
And whoever started them, I'm coming for you
In Bloom
Blooming, like a rose extends its petals to kiss the sun above
I will rise from the ground once more to feel love,
And say that I am sorry, to all.
I won't hurt you the way I hurt myself.

The Fifth Horseman

I know he controls them all. He does not know I know, but I do.
They all reek of his intent. The mean no plan of aid or care. It's
easier to smear someone when you lock them in hospital and
label them with diagnosis. They lose credibility.
This was his plan from the beginning: when his claws were out
of me, he sunk them into any I would reach for. Few escaped
that grip, and the ones that I provided the severance myself,
willing or not.
They call this crazy, or sickness. I am not sick - I see all. I see
through the schemes of demons and heathens, as successful they
are, I see them. I will not be lied to or deterred; I will speak.
Scream. Shriek.
The truth cannot be undone, and I know all about his secrets.
His falsities and his covers ups.
I have admitted my own. The reckoning is coming. He must do
the same. He is no greater man than I, only more devious, and
knew exactly how to break me first. And how he could stop me
from rising. He pollutes the doctors so they do not help. They
feed all my secrets back to him and he adapts his plans. He is
always one step ahead.
Fine, then, I will not share them.
I will build my plans by myself. He shall hear none of them
until too late. My life is not scripture. And if it is, I am the
author. My route will be steered by third parties no longer.
I am my life.
I am my life.
I am.
I am.
I

The Search

Thoughts can kill
Suicide never spawned from the consideration of life
But the fascination of everything the living can never know,
In search of answer,
'Does it get better?'
Perchance there is another plain:
Where we may walk through a forest
And our pupils are not drawn to the shadows being cast by
nature
Is that our nature?
To focus on the shade of something that has stood in light for
centuries
I contrive to feel the sun, but all that stands around me form
silhouettes that
Drown me, like obsidian paint poured over my eyes
Until light and beauty cannot enter
Perchance,
I was not meant to be put onto this plain
Perhaps there is an abyss that will not blind me
That I can see, touch and hear contentment
Oh,
But how to access it?

I Don't Want to Hate My Friends Anymore

I don't want to hate my friends anymore. Or my family. Or my
brothers. Or my sisters. Or the strangers on the street. Or the
nice man who served me coffee. Or the past. Or the future. Or
the present. Or myself. I want to love.
I want to enjoy the trivial moments. The first draw of a
cigarette. The pressing of the pen to the blank page. The first sip
of a cold beer. The warmth of fleeting eye contact.
But these are all pointless. These are necessary evils. The
remembrance of contentment now gone from these minute
pleasures makes them worse.
When they had weight. When they brought joy to my eyes.
Now they only heave in detest, they only perceive what could
bring further agony to what is already dismal and disarrayed.
I burn. I bleed. I plead with a God I don't believe in to
relinquish me from the Devil that I do.
When did the mornings become so lack-luster? At what point
did it become an Olympic task to fill the afternoon with
anything other than thoughts of implosion? When did the pillow
become poison for an already toxic head?

My senses are desolate. Void of anything other than what they
are given via internal lies. I am lost. I am lost. I am lost. I am
lost. I am lost in hurricane of equilibrium that I am safe within
my storm of resentment, yet would be brutalised by any attempt
to venture out. I cannot invite those I can see forward towards
me in fear of them being blown away, or worse, make it through
to me. Such an event would only disappointment them and
enrage me.

I'm sorry. I'm sorry. I'm sorry. I'm sorry.
I wish I was in isolation but such a thing has not existed for
years. Loneliness tastes better than harming reality. But real
loneliness would taste better than this harming illusion.
Torturing mirage, could you just fuck off?
The only way to kill my problems is to destroy my own
conscious.

There is no other, no matter how much I lie to myself.
I am the pestilence of everyone I love. Of everyone I touch. Of everyone I come close to.
I am the wraith.

Sensory Disconnection (ii)

I am transparent,
I am transcending,
All conversation enters and escapes,
Before I can grasp,
Get any hold,
Any anchor,
Away from my despondence.

VI

The Healing

Every sinner has a future,
Every hero has a past,
Every devil had a halo,
Every saint had a confession,
Every death has an impact
But
Not Every life is lived,
Yours can be.

Acceptance

Bad days will always happen. Hold them with no regard when they are over, they will come again. That's life. It's not even mental health, it's just life. Think of them as the days when you appreciate the good days that much more, a reminder of how far you've come. An emotional detox for gratitude. It's good to cry, it's a reminder of our humanity.
This goes further than bad days however. Just like them, we cannot begrudge mental illness. It will spite us in return, and devour us moreover than before. Blaming yourself is toxic, as is blaming the lottery of bad luck. Dwelling on diagnoses or bringing anger to your introspection will only burn you more. The old cliché goes that we can never move forward without first accepting the problem, but accepting must be down with some level of peace. Come to terms with mental health without loathing or bitterness, but open yourself to what life has done. There is nothing you can do to remove it from your life, except carry on your life.
It's a bit like putting up with a family member you don't like when they come to stay. You have to be civil, and at times you'll get in each other's way and it'll be horrible, but there's time you get to spend apart that you'll enjoy far more due to the freedom you have from the situation. The bad days have to be tolerated and the good days have to be witnessed. Again, clichéd, but you can never progress while in denial. And you may never heal from mental illness. But you can certainly grow in spite of it. Winning is when you're happy despite the bad days. You can win.
You will win.

Routine

One of the main ingredients for maintaining stability in my mental health is keeping routines. This involves set times for certain things, and a list of things to do at certain times. Here's what I do each morning:
- I get up at 7:30am every day
- I write something, anything, and put it on a post it notes on my mirror to come back to
- I down a glass of water and make green tea
- I go to the gym or do Yoga depending on how I am feeling
- I do my shower routine
- I make a coffee
- I dress with clothes selected the night before
- I do some breathing
- I start the day

The morning routine can be hard, especially if I don't fall asleep until 5am, but I always feel better after it and feel it sets me up for a productive day. I include my own 'rituals' as I call them, which help me concentrate on being present, for example using loose leaf tea or filter coffee and focusing on making a good brew, instead of rushing and half arising. There might not be much taste difference and it might make me look like a snob, but focusing on the small acts helps me remain present in what I'm doing. I find menial tasks make my mind go places it shouldn't.

It's also really helpful when I have plans. If I have a lecture at 9am it gives me just enough time to do everything and feel energised and hungry for the day. If I don't have a lecture until 1pm, or I have the day off, it means I generally feel better in the morning than without, and less guilty than I would if I had stayed in bed.

It's definitely not a cure for a bad day, and most mornings I wake up incredibly depressed or half functioning, but by setting a different pace in the same routine I can at least bring myself some alleviation by doing things that can help, even if it doesn't feel like it in the moment - which it rarely does, I fucking despise treadmills.

Sticking to a daily or weekly system can have enormous benefits on mental health, and if it doesn't make you feel better, then it might at least make you more productive in your functionality. It can be as drastic or simple as you like. When I first started the only thing on my checklist was to shower before noon, which broke often. It's about starting small and building up, and it should never be stressful - just helpful.

The thing I've found with routines is that they are guaranteed to break at some point. That's okay. It's not the end of the world, it's just a little slip. I once had the slightest break in my routine and it led to my second hospitalisation. Of course, there were other things going on but that was the last straw. Use it as guideline, not a tablet of tone which must be followed to the letter every second. It's okay to treat it like this of course, but it's also okay if it breaks.

Life gets in the way, hangovers and lay in's, holidays or trips away from your own space, shops being closed so you can't get more lavender and chamomile tea, there are always factors that will break the cycle at some point. I think a key thought for keeping the routine going is to always remind yourself why you are doing it. If you do exercise, think about why you do it. If you read a lot, think about why. It's easy to lose emotional connection to an action - which is where motivation is lost and doubt is gained.

One of the things that really helps me, particularly on a day I have nothing to do, is every night I go on an app called ToDoist, which is very simply a to-do list maker on your phone and I set three things for the next day. It could be:

- Uni
- Write Book
- Draw Something

Or on a day off something like:
- Write a poem
- Research use of Psychedelics in Spirituality
- Spend twenty minutes outside

A simple checklist that feels good to complete, and is relatively easy. (Also, on the App every completed item gives you points which is a fantastic source of self-inflation).

Another few things that might be a useful 'destressifier':
- Choose clothes for the next day before bed, it's easier to have it ready and a lot quicker/less stressful than going through options for half an hour each morning.
- Read something, doesn't have to be a book, if concentration is a problem just google 'haiku's about...' and pick your poison. A few words might make you see something you'd never noticed before.
- Make at least one meal, simple or complex, just make sure it's something you actually want to eat
- Find something to replace Facebook, you can't focus on your own thoughts if you're worrying about how people you knew 5 years ago are having kids or have great jobs, if you're thinking about their life in regards to your own and not as two separate things, it's best not to think about.
- Keep your hygiene up, this can be really difficult if you're struggling but you will feel better. Make brushing your teeth into a little fuck you to mental illness.

If routines and lists aren't your thing, maybe just try taking more time to focus on something simple. Treat yourself to making a really good coffee, experiment a little with cooking. Just do it for yourself. And focus on it.

Exercise

I don't want to dwell long on the overused phrase of how a healthy body creates a healthy mind, but there is no denying the two fractions of ourselves are connected. Finding the motivation to exercise or move is a complete effort in itself, particularly on our darkest days, or even when we are a little tired. Determination must be born from the correct origins. If you want to hit the gym or take up yoga in order to change your appearance and love your body a little more, chances are you will not find contentment through this ordeal. At worst, you may self-critique yourself consistently until you give up due to dissatisfaction, or at best you may develop an obsession which could prove itself even more damaging to your mental health if your fire ever burns out.
Exercise for your mind. Think of it as pushing the mind and body into discomfort as training for the difficult days. If you can force yourself to be active for half an hour a day, you'll build a tolerance to that feeling of distaste. The post-sweat satisfaction will always outweigh the initial upstart pains of starting to exercise.

And with that said, there is no correct way to exercise your body and mind. Yoga can be incredibly relaxing for some, and thoroughly enjoyable - but may be a strenuous stretching torture for others. There are so many ways to keep active- swimming, dancing, cycling, hiking - it's vital to pick something that you may not enjoy at the start, but you can see yourself enjoying further down the line. An activity you want to pursue. That's all exercise should be. A fun habit - not a shredding mission for the beach body. Everyone already has a beach body already. There are far more important things to be active for. Exercise the body to aid the mind, the physical stress can bring emotional release.

The Hypocrisy of Running (Don't Lie About Loving It)

I sweat 15 seconds into waking,
And I sweat 15 minutes after rising
Running is a mind-set, and not one I've broken into,
But I feel it will break me soon
My lungs heave and my legs ache
I'm fucking knackered and it's not even eight:

Fuck this fuck this fuck this fuck this fuck this Fuck this fuck
this fuck this fuck this fuck this Fuck this fuck this fuck this
fuck this fuck this Fuck this fuck this fuck this fuck this fuck
this Fuck this fuck this fuck this fuck this fuck this Fuck this
fuck this fuck this fuck this fuck this Fuck this fuck this fuck
this fuck this fuck this Fuck this fuck this fuck this fuck this
fuck this Fuck this fuck this fuck this fuck this fuck this Fuck
this fuck this fuck this fuck this fuck this Fuck this fuck this
fuck this fuck this fuck this Fuck this fuck this fuck this fuck
this fuck this Fuck this fuck this fuck this fuck this fuck this
Fuck this fuck this fuck this fuck this fuck this Fuck this fuck
this fuck this fuck this fuck this Fuck this fuck this fuck this
fuck this fuck this Fuck this fuck this fuck this fuck this fuck
this Fuck this fuck this fuck this fuck this fuck this Fuck this
fuck this fuck this fuck this fuck this Fuck this fuck this fuck
this fuck this fuck this Fuck this fuck this fuck this fuck this
fuck this Fuck this fuck this fuck this fuck this fuck this fuck
this fuck this fuck this fuck this fuck Hiscock this fuck this fuck
this fuck this fuck Hiscock this fuck this fuck this fuck this fuck
Hiscock this fuck this fuck this fuck this fuck Hiscock this fuck
this fuck this fuck this fuck Hiscock this fuck this fuck this fuck
this fuck this Fuck this fuck this fuck this fuck this fuck this
Fuck this fuck this fuck this fuck this fuck this Fuck this fuck
this fuck this fuck this fuck this Fuck this fuck this fuck this
fuck this fuck this Fuck this fuck this fuck this fuck this fuck
this Fuck this fuck this fuck this fuck this fuck this Fuck this
fuck this fuck this fuck this fuck this Fuck this fuck this fuck
this fuck this fuck this Fuck this fuck this fuck this fuck this
fuck this Fuck this fuck this fuck this fuck this fuck this Fuck
this fuck this fuck this fuck this fuck this Fuck this fuck this this
fuck this fuck this fuck this fuck this Fuck this fuck this fuck
this Fuck this fuck this fuck this fuck this Fuck this fuck this
fuck this fuck this fuck this Fuck this fuck this fuck this -
Oh,
It's done
That wasn't so bad
(It absolutely was).

Something to Remember, Always (III)

No one cares about how you look nearly as much as you do.
Take comfort in their apathy. Look how you want to.
You're the only one that can.

Self Esteem & Self Worth

These are inherently different things. Self-esteem may be classed as how you feel about yourself, your confidence and yourself consciousness. Your Self Worth MUST be treated as a different matter altogether. Self-Worth might be seen as how you view yourself in relation to other people - but more importantly, how you allow other people to treat you. This must be focussed and valued above other things. You cannot grow yourself if you allow others to put you down. When trauma is involved, it's increasingly difficult to associate the actions people take with their inherent moral value. You cannot let anyone manipulate you due to your tribulations. You would never tell anyone they deserved to be put down by another person, or value people over each other. Never let anyone do this to you.

Self Esteem is built through a process of trial and error and self-love. It takes a long time to stay consistent (I myself am not close to a life lacking in self-consciousness yet), but it can be practiced by doing what you love for yourself, and for no other reason. To practice prioritising your momentary and long-term needs over the needs of anyone else. Calming the mind, and finding ways not to hate yourself. Read. Meditate. Go out. Wear clothes you want to wear. No one cares about things you do as much as anxiety will tell you. There's a lot of comfort in that; it means your life is yours, to be lived for you.

Habitual Creatures

We spend our lives in training. At the end of Military training you become a Soldier, trained to fight. Any new employment requires sufficient appropriate training. Coping with mental health, in any form, also takes training - but is usually much harder to come by. There are thousands of ways to 'improve your mental health' listed online, but all these checklists forget the crucial mark that maintenance is the hardest part. Even when you start, it's easy to fall off the wagon, you skip one part of your new improvement routine after two days (the usual duration of my self-salvation attempts), then another, and finally the new life of feeling fab is gone. Things like healthy eating and exercise are of course vital to balancing mental health, but they are excruciating to stick at the beginning. The new plan is fresh and exciting, but soon becomes tiring and too much effort. My mistake in the past when starting self-help campaigns is being overzealous, attempting to hit all problems at once. "The voices talk about my weight so I need to diet. Also, women will think I'm ugly unless I work out every day. Also, my mood changes all the time so I need to meditate every day to balance that out. Also, I need to get out of bed earlier and be more productive. Also, I don't like it when people touch my neck so I need to stop freaking out about that, maybe by letting somebody touch my neck and being brave. Also..."

Habit building does not work like this. CBT does not work like this. When engaging in therapy, the patient (usually) works to deal with one problem at a time, gradually building up into a sort of snowball effect when they say 'Goodbye, I feel great now', or something to that effect. Habit building is the same. Introduce one new routine into your life at a time, say once a month. This means you have a new routine being implemented 12 times per annum, and are dedicating a whole month to finding space for the new activity into your daily motions. Twelve habits added in a year is helpful, easier to manage and a stronger goal than a) not doing anything, or, b) doing 23 things for 3 consecutive days and plummeting back on yourself. The aim of a new routine is to make it as seamless as possible to transition into a habitual act incorporated into your daily movements, so that the progression of the build seems effortless. However, it takes a while to fully condition your mind and body. For example, if you embark on a new exercise regime, the body needs to take it slow in order for it to cope with its new tasks - I might argue that the act of going to the gym is more vital than the workout, in that your mind and body condition themselves into being present in the gym, without focusing on a strenuous working. Start simple, a task so easy it seems pointless. When the reality of its simplicity kicks in, begin to build from there - the blocks have been built, the habit can undergo further construction.

Setting goals can also be helpful and rewarding. It feels nice to tick something off of a list, plus some self-constructed pressure can make you work harder towards a goal. So instead of aimless gambits such as; 'I want to cook more', set yourself the challenge of cooking for yourself 3 times in a week - or even only once. Set the goal and make sure you hit it for the first while, and then make a new goal, one slightly more challenging. Give yourself a reward when you hit a target. Little steps are the first phase of big changes.

The most important thing to remember is not too rush. Habits and routines end, but are less likely to if you build it up slowly - and enjoyable. It will be much more difficult to push yourself into a routine you hate.

Recovery is a process: respect it, ritualise it and rejuvenate yourself - but take your time.

The road gets nicer to walk on the further down you get.

Trends in Good Days

Often, I find patterns attaching to good days, routines develop
security between daily transitions, and momentary choices leave
hours stabilised (most of the time). There will always exist the
flinch in decisions, between challenging yourself toward
motivation or shying away. People forget there is comfort in
instability. Depression is painful, but also a painkiller. It wants
to keep you; stay in bed, eat shit, ignore your friends, compare
yourself on Instagram.

Comfort may be the wrong word, but ease is. It's so much easier
to choose a self-destructive path than to maintain the inspired
feeling of change. I find the flinch used to happen around 40
times a day, in literally every decision. Usually the flinch led to
no decision being made, making this its own stressful and
delectably relaxing option.

The problem with the flinch is its attraction - why do something
hard when ease - or nothing at all - is an option.

The challenge is crucial to change, and vital to build.

The first part is making the tougher decisions: go to university
instead of staying bed, get a slightly healthier meal deal from
Tesco rather than McDonald's, cook something healthier than a
Tesco meal deal, go to the gym instead of having a smoke, read
instead of binging Netflix, write instead of scrolling Facebook,
sleep instead of starting a film (this one is still a major work in
progress).

Over the past 3 months (3 years, but let's pretend I'm making
fantastically quick progress), challenging the flinch has resulted
in a huge reduction in the number of flinches I experience. The
things that fade from challenges to routines then become
enjoyable (God forbid the gym actually might become a
pleasant experience eventually), and demand be done from
excitement, rather than reluctance and obligation. Thus, here
are, as the chapter title might suggest, some trends in the good
days, and the tough decisions that cause 4 minutes of hatred
followed by a day which appears to be slightly more
manageable.

- Exercising as early as possible
- Writing something as soon as I wake
- Having time on my own before seeing anyone
- Delaying and withholding phone usage
- Meditation
- Cooking
- Cold shower in the morning, hot shower before bed
- Making nice coffee instead of a) buying one, or b) making a shit instant one
- Drawing
- Stretching lots
- Going between things regularly, rather than stranding myself to one job for a day
- Working on something for myself (there's is meter high pile of lyrics, songs, poems and drawings no one, including me, will ever see, and that's a nice thought in the moment - stop focusing on the end goal and just remember the process of being creative)

Trends, habits, routine, ritual - whatever self-help glossary you read from will preach forward (hark on about) how vital structure is to build healthy habits and a contented lifestyle. It's not all bollocks. Routine takes a long time to aggrandise itself into a noticeable and palatable experience - consistently it may feel like far more effort than small tasks will seem - but carry through. The more your passion moves the further you move from illness.

Give yourself a shot. You're the only person who can.

Saturation

Oh, You are blitzkrieg,
Ravaging my mind nightly,
Oh yes, you are Spartan,
With iron will, held high and mighty.
You are brutal and savage,
You are clarity, river like,
You drown me.
You are sunlight,
Make my passion burn through insufferable woe's.
You are exposure turned too bright or too dim,
Never allowing me any clear picture to view.
You are heaven where I bathe for hours,
You are hell, where I am condemned for eternity.
You are freedom, from ever a dull moment.
You are chains, binding me to the forgotten lore of a slave.

Though I rise in my ranks. You are nothing compared.
You are part of me - I am the full definition.
You may be Capital Letter but I am Sentence and Full Stop.
You affect only the font of this tale.
It will be my hand that writes.

Expression

Without attempting (but failing to hide) an obvious plug, my band Incarnate. has been the greatest therapy I have ever undertaken. Through lyrics and performance, I have found myself able to cleanse myself of fury and guilt every few weeks at our gigs. It is a place - not a band, for me, a place, in which I can expose, reveal and express my darkest thoughts, trauma and daily tribulations and force people to listen. The music may make people uncomfortable, as with the performance - and so it should. If a person can walk away from hearing a set of songs about sexual abuse, psychosis, fregoli delusion, suicide and self-immolation with a smile on their face and having loved every hook we have failed. I want to connect, to entertain a spectrum of emotions, not play cool tunes to cool people. I want to burn the hearts, to impact the souls of those that witness - to spurn and to heal others who may identify in those lyrics of intoxication. It is a place for honesty without regret. A place of sanctuary through devils, a place for the demons to thrive and it be called 'art'. My mental clarity has endeavored to progress through this project, and each performance becomes a ritual of devotion; that is, devotion to self-betterment, to rid my head of its worst poisons, to use pain for betterment, to develop myself. Suffering is cultivated and explodes into the eyes and ears of our witnesses; our souls go into the hands of friends and viewers. It is a place of trust that I have known only in fleeting moments, with full control in how deep my explanations may be fathomed.

I am most likely, incredibly biased towards creative outlets as an artist, but I cannot express the value of expression, or expulsion, through artistic medium's enough. It is never too late to begin a creative endeavor, in any way or form. Tell a story about yourself through photographs, make mental plague's a reality through acting or film making, explore dance as a form of self-betterment and release. Nothing will focus or content your mind more than relinquishing your thoughts to a poem or song. Creativity breeds exploration and progression - in my opinion there is no better way to better your mind than to exercise it through expression. It allows you to portray your most extensive and hurtful truths without directly talking. It is liberation. Try. Who cares if what you do is shared with other people? It should only be for you.

Sound tracking

I am (with some bias) a great believer that music has some of the greatest influence on our mood. From sing-alongs in the car filled with joy, to aggressive rhythms to fuel the antagonisation of exercise, to soothing harmonies to find relaxation - the songs we listen to can perhaps be some of the greatest influencers on our mood in the present moment. You can find solace, company and understanding who a lyricist you just seem to get you, or the animalistic drumming of a heavy band might help you find catharsis in your rage.

However, I think it's easy to listen to the 'wrong' music - by which I mean music that might negatively impact or math your mood. If you find yourself wallowing in somber verses more often that playing tunes that might pull you out of a low mood, it may not be healthy. While it's vital to find understanding and community through musical art, it risks becoming easy to ignore the fact that a sad song may be progressing your sadness. Of course, it could never be as simple as this, but I always find certain songs consistently make me smile or move or cry and or scream in a way no others do, and it's such a simple way or releasing emotion or elevating mood.

220

I was going to share my choices but I think it's important that everyone have their individual selects. Maybe take some time to make a playlist of songs that might drag you towards a brighter mood, or just alleviate some of the heaviness from your mentality. Light songs, cheesy songs; it's okay to listen to happy music too. It can be good to sing hopeful lyric. It can even be good to dance.

How to Start Healing

The first step, or leap, is the hardest part of recovery. The aim of
the first challenge is to find a way to retain the consistency of
healing - we've all made grand first efforts towards attempting
something, and then failed within a week (every New Year's
resolution, ever). How can we remove the friction from this
initial journey? They say when you quit smoking, the first week
is the hardest, and it's generally slightly plainer sailing the
further down the road you get. I would associate this same ethos
to self-care; it's easy to lost those moments of inspiration
quickly if you haven't set up properly for the inevitable
obstacles that will come.

I think the first step comes in two parts:
1) Planning the first month, in full. Having a schedule or
expansively detailed plan for the entire first 4 weeks makes you
more likely to stick to it - you can see what you've done, what
your aiming for, and why you're aiming for it. Make a list of
achievable goals you can do in that first month. Make them
versatile but not intensive, they need to be easily manageable to
ensure you can tick them off. Ticking the goals off always
brings an air of accomplishment - so why not cheat and make as
many easy ones as you can. Pride yourself of the small tasks
before building to the big ones. You can aim to have bigger
challenges (whatever they may be, they must be individual;
maybe to join a gym, finish a book, go to the doctor, spend time
with friends for a full day) nearer the end of this first term, but
your confidence should be grown before then. Even if you feel
confident before the end of the first four weeks, take time to
make sure you're really okay with smaller tasks, maybe such as
eating every day or spending an hour away from technology,
before you progress to things that may prove to be more
extreme.

There is no shame or limit in how tiny your aims can be. If it's just to get out of bed two days in a row, that's sensational. Your progression can never be compared to someone else's. You're only doing this for you, so do it for you in a way you want to. No one else's plan will work for you in full (of course, elements may be used and prove hugely beneficial) but you have to adapt to your own life and your own needs.

Ensure there's nothing coming up in the first couple of weeks that might throw you off course, and if there is, try and cancel it. If you can't cancel, go with precautions in place - a way to leave early, or perhaps take some sort of stress reliever with you. Go boldly, even when you're unprepared, you will surprise yourself.

If you're struggling to keep up with your listed aims, part two may bring some comfort:

2) Hope for the best but be open to the worst. The more open minded you are to failing or falling back on your mission, the less likely you are to do so. Build your pace slowly, do not expect bad days to suddenly stop. They won't, and that's okay. It's a journey where you can focus on the small victories - don't create an endgame just yet, or if you have an idea of one, make sure you're planning it to be in the distance. It may come quicker than anticipated, but be ready for a long road of progression. Never put pressure on yourself to make progress quickly. It may take a long time, and that's okay. The long road is what we're aiming for, and you can focus on the glimpses of clarity on that road as you walk down it. If you only focus on the end goal, you'll never reach it. Be aware of your constant development, encourage yourself and be gentle when you struggle. Progress has been made already, which is a huge achievement. You're always allowed to celebrate.

Burnout can happen quickly and suddenly if these preparations have not been made. And if it comes regardless, forgive and move on. Dwelling on the fact you've exhausted yourself will exhaust you more. Acknowledge the burnout and move on, take it slower and allow it to be a bad day. They will always happen - you're trying to reduce the frequency that mental health impacts you - not erase it entirely, this is not possible. Merely reassess, adapt and move forward. It's okay.

It may be a good idea to tell someone close to you that you're making this effort of self-love. Even if you're not asking for aid, a listening ear is always welcomed for you to tell your discoveries and tribulations to, to describe the battles you've won and to hear the things you've struggled with most. You can explore your own journey through describing it to someone - perhaps leading to a sort of reviewed analysis where you can highlight what's working and what's hardest. You may want to ask for help in certain things. Requesting someone to join you on a doctor's trip, or help you eat healthy etc. Do it. Almost everything in life is easier when it is shared with another.

I'd recommend documenting the first few weeks regardless, in order to keep track of your progress. This can be done through any form, via bullet points, a journal, or any way you're most comfortable with. I find it really helps to look back at daily and weekly reviews in order to recognise any similarities in bad days and what may have brought them on, i.e. lack of sleep, or a specific event, or if it's just Monday's (Tuesday's for myself). By keeping track of your daily habits and moods you can identify these red areas much easier, and adapt from them as you progress.

Drink water. Eat plenty. Focus on the better days.
Be proud of yourself.

The Waste

The reoccurrence of episodes and impacted day takes its toll with feelings of neglect and disappointment. I track in my journal and daily reviews my condition: I analyse the common factors in bad days and avoid them where possible, I put more energy into the repeated traits of the good days. I feel I have an abundance of introspection, but I'm blind to any permanence. It proves impossible thus far to forgive bad days when I work so hard to negate them. I fail to remind myself that they cannot be completely refuted, they are a part of this process, they will always be inevitable.

As much as I find myself able to cope with the emotional states I am dragged to, my anger is directed elsewhere. Rather than a feeling of coping, I find fury in the wasted time my mind steals me from; time that could have been spent on self-betterment or work. It becomes difficult to remember that breaks are needed from work, and my productivity will never flow the same way as it does when I am motivated as to when I am low, but this is what frustrates me. As someone who prides themselves on spending most hours of the day working in some description, I can only look back and see the empty hours documented, angry that I could not find ways to fill them. When you've began to take pride in your ability for health self-medication and skills in self-care, idleness can bring a feeling of powerlessness, a hollow breeze of failure that seeps into my head.

I find myself needing to incredibly remind myself this is not laziness. This is the process, the path, the persistence that I have no choice but oblige and allow. If I've only had 3 mornings off this week to relax, then an afternoon and evening can be permitted to dedicating time to resting and recovering. The efforts in productivity may be my distraction, but sometimes we must face those darker parts. I must sit in them when I have no other choice. Allow the break and let it inspire the next few days. Focus that these periods of beigeness and toil are now less frequent, and serve as a reminder as to why I must distract myself so intensely. If these times must demand to be suffered, then I demand to be as relentless in my efforts when they are gone, I will burn brighter than they can douse.

We must not dwell on our previously wasted days, nor focus on the limited of number of hours ahead, but only focus on what we require in the very present moment - this is the only way to look back with contentment. To be able to think 'I did exactly what I needed'. That is all life is.

Losing Apathy

The assumption of apathy has become an incredulously easy task in the current state of affairs. When the world is regarded as completely fucked by most people (and let's face it, the world is definitely completely fucked), it's become so much easier to just switch off from the political noise and social hysteria. Focusing on one's life is definitely a valuable task, and always more important than focusing on the stress being vomited to us via the media. The news is depressing, politics and modern democracy are absolute jokes, we're deluded into believing inequality is a far less significant issue than. it is, and there seems to be an ever-increasing generational rift, with everybody losing patience with everybody.

Anger is better than apathy. Anger can be fuel, driving confidence and creativity. When the world becomes numb and cruel, when we believe hope is lost for whatever culture we now find ourselves in, this is when individuals are born. I am a believer in the importance of taking time away from the world when it becomes too much, our minds need detox time. When bad news is a constant stream through every news outlet perhaps this is the moment to use apathy for betterment. Switch off from scrolling and the deafening noise of real-time broadcasting, focus on your own life, your own eyes. Focus on everything you can see on your journey and the things that are actually important in your own, individual life. Realise that life does not revolve around white people in suits on the news, it revolves around whatever you make it. Less noise leads to sharpened sight.

Breaking away from the events that don't impact your own experiences is a healthy task to undertake, one that prove effective and efficient in building a more focused life. Perhaps we could suggest this to be a sort of essentialist or minimalist approach to what information we choose to take in to streamline our thoughts, allowing us to concentrate on what truly matters in life.

With that said, nonchalance to life should maybe a short term and occasionally visited practice. If you practice in any creative expression, there's a large chance the planet's impending doom will present itself some muse to you. Perhaps we hold a responsibility to re-engage with the life outside of ourselves, to connect with the strife of our greater community - humanity. After all, if we ignore the stresses for too long, the guilt of this may become a factor, or we become too focused in our own minds and forget those outside it. However, if you find contentment in the quiet, crash on and follow that, I'm sure it will guarantee a far more peaceful life.

But if you cannot shake the itch of the world's pain, do not shake it. Be open about your discomfort and discontent; fight stigma, break this cycle of silence that has been etched into us. There is no such thing as a normal life anymore; do what you want, and love it.

Anger is passion. Passion is a fantastic push for almost any ailment.

If you've found the apathy you feel is towards yourself, with lack of care to your own internal being, externalise your thoughts. Get out of your own brain and focus on those you love, the things that demand your attention in the most joyous way. As hard as it is when the scales are tilted - it does mean that the more you detest yourself the more you can appreciate the things outside yourself, and via those things that draw you can learn to lose the apathy for yourself, and re-discover the passion you hold for your soul.

Discovering Passion

Hunger gives us everything. Our hunger for food provides us with life and energy, cravings feed us pleasurable taste. Hunger for 'success' brings motivation and opportunity, an animalistic urge that takes hold until effort has not been spent in despair or vain. Passion is easy to be burn through or become frustrated with - it is a being that always brings expectations and dreams, as well as obstacles. Often there is more difficulties than release, but when relief comes, it unloads any of those previous burdens. Passion does not necessarily have to adhere to your career plan or any specific hobbies, but only your craving to live life. I find mental illness has always made me hungry. In my darkest hours, even after surviving suicide attempts, I have felt more connected with myself and life than ever before. Perhaps relating to a 'better get on with it then' attitude, or genuine inspiration, the weeks after this point have often been the most fruitful in the slow development of the early recovery stages; laying the groundwork, making clear aims, building plans, solutions, and deterrents. Though the most vital parts of this stage is to make the plans accessible during relapses and blips - to ensure I never end up at exactly square one. Square two or three is fine, as long as some progress has been made. Otherwise it's easy to convince yourself all those plans were mere delusion.

So how do we stay hungry for healing when we're at our worst? The bad news is that if any of us knew, long standing mental health issues wouldn't exist, as we'd solve them after a single blip. The good news, however, is that this leaves a vast reservoir of experimentation to explore through life. Human's love learning - we spend our entire lives in education, whether through an organised system or not, we constantly seek new information. If this was false, we wouldn't engage in new hobbies or career paths as we grew older, or visit new places or learn languages, or take up instruments or even meet people. We are inherently fascinated by that in which we have no idea of. We can use this, harness it as a tool in the arsenal against diagnosis and doubt. Interest peaks in our exploration of self-discovery and engagement with ourselves - the more we understand ourselves fundamentally, the more we can control our internal environment, surely? Thus, leading to a conclusion where, through constant experimentation on systems that work for you as a person or as a stabiliser for your mental health, then you can gradually, but undoubtedly, develop a self-protection system for yourself - and with the ability to constantly adapt it to your ever-changing circumstance.

Knowledge is power, but relentless hunger for that knowledge is the real aid in battle. If you can stay inspired, you cannot be beaten.

Breathing Space

This breathing space, however, need not always need to be looked for in nature alone. I think it's vital to establish your own breathing space that's easily accessible every day, without fail. A place where the primary objective is to relax and forget the over bearing pressures for life. This could be your favourite local coffee shop, a park, maybe even your bed. It should be individual, and above all, personal. Like your little secret haven of quite you can escape to when needed. Though perhaps it's first easier to dissociate this special location from others - to create its separate entity by creating other unique spaces. I tend to be able to work wherever I am, whether while travelling or at a mate's house, I, like most in Western Society, have become increasingly haunted by the guilty conscious of productivity, which follows many of us everywhere. Constantly feeling like we should be hustling or working or doing something that isn't eating bread and watching Netflix. And even if the latter is what consumes our time - we are bound to feel guilty about the lost hours that could have been spent striving towards some goal. I think this comes from a plethora of origins; the competition of modern life displayed on social media, the unbearable pressure of working towards a future that's looking inevitably fucked anyway, and the seemingly-natural self-hatred that we induce into ourselves for not being a superhuman. Our lives become endangered when our time off work is plagued by the consequences of not working.

For some, it may be easier to dedicate a singular working space for themselves, the only place, or couple of locations, where they permit themselves to work exclusively. Maybe a room in your home; a room where the only real reason to sit in it is to work, and when you're not in it, you don't. However, maybe a room in the home makes it too easy to continue working at all times, particularly when more and more people are working freelance or from home, thus leading to it becoming more difficult to increase friction between home and work. So perhaps it's better, for you, to choose somewhere not in the home, but still easily accessible. Coffee shops, libraries, art galleries can all become attractive options.

I personally find it easier to exclude places rather than dedicate a particular working space. Due to the nature of my working being relatively easy to undertake while on the move, I sort of refuse to negate these opportunities for graft; even if I'm relaxing with friends but working on my laptop, I enjoy being productive while relaxing. However, while I allow myself to work most places, I follow a self-made law of the places I cannot work. For example, I have a cushion and a coffee table in my flat that rises about a foot off the floor. This is the only place when home I allow myself to work. It's ideal for me, as with my concentration level I tend to float between 6 jobs at once, and I tend to time which I'm working on depending on if my back or bum are aching from too long on the floor. When this occurs, a quick stretch or 10 minutes of yoga is undertaken, and then I resume my task for another short burst. I never allow myself to work in my bed; it's a place that I reserve as much as possible for sleep alone, and if I don't sleep, I lie on the floor and try to relax there. I find it easier to relax and breathe on a floor (it's actually my ideal breathing space/place to relax), so if I can relax myself enough, hopefully I can sleep when I go back to the bed.

I tend to divide my room into 'sections' for different things. A corner for clothes and a mirror, the only place where I let myself worry about clothes or things to that affect, otherwise it'll ruin my day. A section for work as mentioned, which has a very simple set up of my laptop, notebooks and some stones, and then the rest of the room is reserved for my own headspace. For yoga, for reading, for watching films or for writing music (I find it impossible to undertake this in my work space), it's the 'me-area'. I can step in and switch off my phone and generally feel content to be in that space.

I'd greatly encourage anyone struggling with their mental health to undertake a similar practice, or to just choose a place to either work or relax and to be as strict as possible in sticking to the rules you create. The modern world work obsession is only conducive to the degradation of mental health. And while we may not be able to change how society runs itself (yet) we can at least fight how it impacts us. If the world is designed to drown us, we must design our own little Islands where we can catch our breath.

The Serenity of Nature

It is no new FAD that spending time outdoors is good for the human soul - the great wildernesses have been the natural human habitat for thousands of years, only recently (in the grand scheme of our existence) have we come to spend almost all of our times indoors.

I find nature to be one of the most calming retreats for the mind to take respite and refuel, with fresh air and views which offer a greater perspective than the hum-drum of stress-inducing city life. Having spent most of my life living in the East Coast of beautiful Scotland, I always took for granted how important the surroundings were to me until I moved to the behemoth of Manchester - a relatively (at least for me) colossal field of huge grey buildings and people with no time. Only after moving to heart of a big city did I realise how much I needed greenery around me, which my new life initially was holding a severe lack of.

It's scientifically proven that spending time outdoors has huge benefits for our mental health, I think the problem for most of us is to find the accessibility of it. It can be relatively easy to find big parks or walks around to waste a day away from the city in, it might just take a little bit of research in how to find this breathing space.

Stepping Away

This is the final chapter. I want to start with that, because my
ability to concentrate might run out very soon and my ability to
keep working on this is taking its toll on me. I'm in a better
place now than I was, and these words remind me of the places I
have been. So, I'll say farewell now, in case I shut the laptop
and never open it again.

My circumstances have improved dramatically since I started
writing this, something which I count as a blessing every day.
However, that is not to say my mind doesn't still hurt and haunt
me, or my skull feels like it's under corrosion from my
condition every day. The days are better. Maybe I am too. It's
hard to tell sometimes. I've done my best to follow my own
advice while writing this, and I can definitely say it's helped me
put some stabilisers on my life. For almost a year now, my bad
days have not hospitalised me - which may not sound like much,
but is actually a colossal milestone for me. I couldn't have done
it without the people around me, and who I have been around
for the past year, however big or small a role they played it my
life. I'm also proud of myself, for not giving up on the future
when I wanted to. And grateful to whatever luck there is the
world, that stopped me when I had.
For the first time in years, I'm excited for the future. I have no
clue what will come, how long I'll live and still if I'm even
alive. If this will ever be read by anyone that isn't me. I hope so.
It hurt a lot.
But that's okay.
I guess that's what life is, and what recovery is.
You get to a point where all the pain is okay. Still breathing,
heart still beating, still alive. I'm sure of it.
Maybe that's what healing is.

And I'm not saying I am healed, fucking hell no. No, I'm only a few steps into the road of recovery. But it's getting nicer. The steps feel lighter and less strenuous. And there are still frequent roadblocks, but there always will be. These are chronic illnesses.
And that is okay. No life is perfect. That is okay.

Thank you. For reading this. I hope you learned and felt and experienced something. I hope it's a bit clearer that we're not that different, despite our realities. If not, sorry. That's my bad, not yours. Thank you for spending some time with me in this way. I appreciate the gesture so much. It takes so much open mindedness and heart to look into someone else's mind and heart. I hope you're okay. That you're doing well. Or that you can see the wellness coming. It is. I hope you're in love. With parts of life. With yourself. With the future.

Dark times, light shines.
Anguished cries, followed by relief.
Perilous road, walk for miles, miles, miles.
Hope always befalls the most broken smiles.

Okay.
That's me.
Thank you.
I wish you all best. You are blessed. You're still here.

Thank you.

I Am, Almost.

We have stopped wishing for our time to be lived in Heaven,
For now, Earth will have to suffice.
There is no use concerning thoughts of Hell or hereafter,
When we are as blind to the unknown as those three wee, daft
and joyous mice.
There is a gift that was given to be lived, whether we wanted it
or not:
We are here now; in the middle of the sandstorm we are caught.
But this tempest need not swallow us whole –
We can fashion goggles and cloaks to shield us from its might.
We can fight, screaming and loving, and reject the blackest of
the nights.
Oh, how the sky may swallow all, the dark can hide stars from
our sight,
But we hath fashioned our armor, we walk forward unto the
light.

These silent voices shriek at the prospect of contentment,
They strive to thrive on our hopelessness, they fill us with
resentment,
They speak of a race where all our fellow brothers and sisters
are contestants.
That we must beat them, be ready to feed on them.
Kill and maim those we cherish and love, disintegrate their
souls when push comes to shove
The voices back. Burn them instead. And though our skulls are
filled with hate, the battle is only in our heads.
A comfort this is not, but perspective it has to offer.
If there are countries outside our eyes, the wars of minds are so
much smaller.
Regret not the time they stole, resent not the words they preach,
Every scar beholds a lesson, proof that vast knowledge is within
your reach. And the road is long, winding and narrow.
Filled with demons of distrust who will mock and surely boast.
But I am positive I have found the correct path, in spite of them.
I am, Almost.

The End.

Acknowledgements

The author would like to acknowledge this book is written entirely based upon personal experiences and that any differences in symptoms are entirely plausible.

Cheers to the voices, I guess. You made this possible.

Huge thanks to my parents for your understanding –
this is only part of this book I'll allow you to read.

I am indebted to Tina McGuff for inspiring me to write this novel through her own extraordinary journey, and I'm so grateful for your wise words and warm smiles while I awkwardly asked for your afternoons. Thank you so much for your honesty and conversation.

I'd also like to give a huge thank you to Lucy Fox for designing the cover of this book. It makes sense as one of my oldest mates you'd know exactly what I wanted. Text me more.

A special thank you to my brothers in Incarnate. Joe, Giannis, Dan, you've all kept me sane more than you know. Thank you for embracing my negative parts and helping me use them for art.
I love you all. Viva Incarnate.

Of course, I owe a massive thank you to everyone in my life who has helped me along this ongoing journey. There are too many people who have helped me for it to be fair to call names. But thank you. Loved Ones. Friends. Family. Folk I've lived with, Doctors, Nurses, Teachers, Strangers. I am the product of my interactions with you all and I'm so grateful to everyone who has shared parts of their lives with me.

Which comes to thanking you. So very much. For reading this and spending your time with me. You humble me.

And finally, I thank you, Ramona.
I truly hope this reaches you somehow.

Spencer Mason is a writer and musician living in Manchester, England. Originally from Broughty Ferry, Scotland, he now studies Songwriting (BA Hons) at BIMM University, and performs as the singer and songwriter of the band Incarnate. (@IncarnateUK), who run the charity event Time to Talk in aid of breaking the stigmatisation and promoting the discussion of mental health. Alongside this he experiments with transferring his writings to various mediums, such as poetry and theatre performances. He uses his personal Instagram to promote his work (@spencer_mason361).